Couldn't Be Better

The story of two people:
one American, one Russian,
and their dream for rural Russia

The Russian Farm Community Project

LaVern "Vern" Freeh

Germans from Russia Heritage Collection
North Dakota State University Libraries
Fargo, North Dakota
2000

Couldn't Be Better

LaVern "Vern" Freeh

Copyright © 2000
Germans from Russia Heritage Collection
NDSU Libraries
P.O. Box 5599
Fargo, ND 58105-5599

Germans from Russia Heritage Collection website:
www.lib.ndsu.nodak.edu/gerrus

Library of Congress Control Number: 00-135782
ISBN 1-891193-17-1

Design and printing in the United States of America
by the Germans from Russia Heritage Collection
North Dakota State University Libraries
Fargo, ND 58105-5599

At the request of the author, the proceeds from the sale of this book will be divided equally between the Russian Farm Community Project, Minneapolis, Minnesota and Moscow, Russia, and the Germans from Russia Heritage Collection at the North Dakota State University Libraries, Fargo, North Dakota.

PRAISE FOR THE RUSSIAN FARM
COMMUNITY PROJECT

"I was able to gain an appreciation of the highly productive work you are doing and to pick up some insights into Russian agriculture as well...I am pleased that we are now supporting your work through our Food for Progress Program."

U.S. Agriculture Secretary, Dan Glickman
at the project site in 1995

"My country can never repay you for what you, the Russian Farm Community Project, and your supporters are doing to assist our rural communities at this time of great need...but rest assured, we are most grateful for those efforts and we shall try in every way possible to demonstrate that your investments in our future, and yours, are well placed."

Russian Ambassador Yuri Vorestosov
addressing RFCP board members in
Washington, D.C. in 1997

"My dream has always been to develop a successful public/ private relationship which will assure the social and economic well-being of the people in my Raion...Through the Russian Farm Community Project, that dream is being realized."

Viktor V. Gravilov, Chief Administrator (Governor)
of Dmitrov to RFCP board members in 1997

"The RFCP dairy initiative truly represents a new beginning for agriculture in this region creating new sources of income, more jobs and greater opportunities for the people of the Dmitrov Raion and equally important more critically needed high quality wholesome milk for the children of the region."

The Honorable James Collins
U.S. Ambassador to Russia
at project site, June, 1999

"A bold experiment...that could spread to other parts of Russia to help this country feed its people abundantly."

Chattanooga Free Press
Chattanooga, TN
May 1, 1994

"They're making progress...more potatoes, better corn and a harvest of goodwill...teaching Russian farmers how to do it on their own..."

Star Tribune
Minneapolis, MN
September 27, 1994

This organization is more than words and promises...it is supported by action and deeds..."

Dmitrov Herald
Dmitrov, Russia
September 10, 1994

"An historic opportunity...agricultural experts are creating a prototype..."

Los Angeles Times
Los Angeles, CA
July 6, 1993

TABLE OF CONTENTS

DEDICATION

This book is dedicated to two people, one an American and one a Russian; one in the twilight of his life, one not yet thirty when the Russian Farm Community Project was launched, who united in a common cause to help rural people in Russia to effectively make the transition from Communism to Capitalism during a time of confusion, uncertainty and turmoil following the sudden collapse of Communism in 1991.

This is a story of what can be done if one has the capacity to dream and the energy, enthusiasm, and support to turn that dream into reality.

This is the story of Ralph Hofstad and Andrei Danilenko, who have been the heart and soul of the Project and through their energy and enthusiasm have inspired others, American and Russian, to catch their passion and be a part of their efforts.

The result has been a Project which, against great odds, has made a significant difference in Russia, and has given new credence to a statement by the famous anthropologist, Margaret Meade, *"Never doubt that a small group of thoughtful committed citizens can change the world, indeed it is the only thing that ever has."*

ACKNOWLEDGMENTS

The author is deeply indebted to Dennis Behl, former Director of Communications of the Russian Farm Community Project, for assisting with the preparation and assembly of much of the information in this book and, along with Tom Hommeyer providing most of the pictures; To Kimberly Hanson, RFCP's office administrator and "do it all" person who took my almost illegible handwritten pages and converted them into clear and legible phrases; And, finally to Dr. Ronald Roskens, The Reverend Dr. Norman Broadbent, The Reverend Dr. Otis Young, Susan Dudas, and Vern Moore, who read the first drafts of the text. To all who helped and supported me in this effort and most especially my wife, Lois. Thank you very much.

Vern Freeh

INTRODUCTION

Before reading this book it is well that you understand what you will be reading. The book is not an in-depth review of Russia and its many problems.

Rather, it is a brief historical sketch of how two highly dedicated people, and those they assembled around them, were able to make a difference in a Russia struggling to find itself following the collapse of Communism.

The author traces the planning which preceded their efforts, the partnerships they formed, the steps they followed in implementing the Russian Farm Community Project; the things they were able to accomplish; the major difficulties they encountered; the lessons learned and, finally, their goals and priorities for the future.

PART I

COLLAPSE, CHAOS AND THE AFTERMATH

THE RISE AND FALL OF COMMUNISM

The Communist system came into being in Russia in 1917 because the nobility (the landowners, people of wealth) ignored the plight of the poor and disenfranchised to the point where they were no longer willing to tolerate their situation.

This set the stage for a group of opportunists to come to the fore-front promising a different form of government and a better way of living where everyone would be treated equally. They promised there would no longer be the very rich or the very poor in Russia, and the needs of all would receive equal attention. And so with the "promised land" before them the people joined with the new opportunists in a revolution against the existing government and the Communist system was put into place. It was to last for 74 years.

Collectivization of Soviet Agriculture[1]

During the first twelve years after the 1917 Bolshevik Revolution, Russian peasants continued to farm their individual parcels except for those who joined a small number of experimental collectives established on lands seized from the large landlords. During the early and mid-1920s, under Lenin's new "Economic Policy," the peasants could even sell their production on the market and were generally free of government crop seizures. The Soviet state, however, continued to own the land, as it had since the 1917 Land Decree. In the late 1920s, things changed dramatically as Stalin began a campaign against the so-called "*kulaks*" (better off peasants). Anyone who farmed more than 30 hectares (one hectare equals 2.47 acres), or had more than three cows, or ran a small shop, or hired any labor was vilified as a *kulak* and enemy of the state.

In 1929, forced collectivization began in earnest. A combination of ideological reasons prompted collectivization, including the desire for state control over the distribution and use of agricultural production and concern for political control of the peasantry. Production plummeted, and Stalin briefly discontinued the collectivization policy in 1930, at which time most farmers left the new collectives. Stalin soon reinstated the policy, however, and completed the collectivization process over the next several years. A simultaneous drive to liquidate the *kulaks*

---

[1]Excerpted from Rural Development Institute #84 "Russian Agrarian Reform: A Status Report from the Field", Roy L. Prosterman and Leonard J. Rolfes, Jr.

2

as a class drove millions of peasants from the land they farmed. The disruption of production was awesome. Farmers slaughtered much of the country's livestock, preferring to butcher them for meat rather than give them to the collectives. More than five million people died in the resulting famine. Resisters were executed.

Changes in Collectivized Agriculture Since the 1930's[2]

At first, virtually all production on the collectively farmed lands was seized by the state to support forced industrialization. The peasants survived, as well as they could, on what they could produce on their tiny household ("private") plots. Then, after Stalin's death in 1953, Nikita Khrushchev liberalized procurement policies, beginning a slow and uncertain revival of incentives for the peasants. In the mid-1960s, state resources began to be poured into the collective and state farm sector in an effort to improve production. These massive expenditures continued until recently.

The size of collective and state farms gradually increased, as smaller farms were combined to form larger ones. When the Soviet Union broke up in 1991, there were approximately 27,000 collective and state farms in the Russian Republic and 50,000 in the Soviet Union. These farms averaged over 4,500 hectares of crop land, even larger amounts of pastureland, and about 400 workers.

The number of state farms grew steadily in relation to collective farms, with the government often taking over financially troubled collectives for direct bankrolling by the government. On the eve of the recent reforms, however, there was little practical difference between the two types of farms. The "election" of collective farm chairmen was largely guided from outside, so there was little difference from the appointment of state farm directors. Collective farm members received a set monthly salary financed out of a line of credit from the state banks regardless of profitability (plus a bonus based on production), making their remuneration essentially indistinguishable from that of state farm workers. Private plots were allowed on both. Retired farmers on both collective and state farms received state pensions.

Collectivized agriculture clearly did not work well in the Soviet Union. Labor productivity was lower (by about a factor of ten) on Soviet farms than in the United States and Canada. Measured most

---

[2]Excerpted from Rural Development Institute #84 "Russian Agrarian Reform: A Status Report from the Field", Roy L. Prosterman and Leonard J. Rolfes, Jr.

comprehensively, total factor productivity in climatically comparable areas of North American agriculture was more than twice that of the Soviet Union. That is, for the same amount of land, material inputs and labor, Soviet farms produced less than half as much as North American farms in similar climatic areas. If the Soviet farms inefficient use of seed and feed is considered, the gap becomes still wider. Private plots, which occupied roughly three percent of the cultivated land in the Soviet Union, produced 25-30 percent of the total value of agricultural production in the country. In addition, Soviet state and collective farms lost 25 percent or more of their production during the harvest and post-harvest processes. As a result, grain had to be imported to help feed a country with sufficient agricultural potential to feed itself. State investment in collective and state farms was heavily subsidized, aggravated by government decisions to write off much of the long-term debt. Soviet collectivized farming proved to be a black hole down which vast resources disappeared and from which little light emerged.

Unfortunately no one could ever imagine in 1917, that the price people would pay for following the Communists was the total surrender of their personal freedom, their possessions, and their initiative to the Communist Party. Those who refused would be uprooted from their homes and families, tortured, imprisoned in Gulags, and killed.

The irony is that after paying such a horrible price the people found that their country still consisted of the "haves" and "have-nots." Only now, the "haves" were the members of the Communist Party.

By the early 1980's the negative consequences of Communist rule were becoming quite apparent in Russia and the entire Soviet Union both of which were showing serious signs of deterioration. The country was near bankruptcy, both financially and philosophically, and its people were largely drained of their initiative and creativity.

Changes Under Gorbachev and Yeltsin[3]

In the late 1980's an agrarian reform process began with the slow emergence of peasant farms. This emergence was encouraged first by Mikhail Gorbachev and others at the all-union level and by the leadership in several republics and districts. Initially these peasant farms emerged without benefit of supporting legal provisions. Starting in 1989 the U.S.S.R. government, and later, the republic governments, began to

---

[3]Excerpted from Rural Development Institute #84 "Russian Agrarian Reform: A Status Report from the Field", Roy L. Prosterman and Leonard J. Rolfes, Jr.

give the peasant farming movement formal recognition. The Russian laws did not mandate a general redistribution of land, but provided two alternative mechanisms for granting farmers land. The first was a shareholding system on collective and state farms by which collective farm members and state farm workers received shares, which could be traded in for plots of land and other assets to establish a peasant farm. The second mechanism created a state land fund from unused and under-utilized land. The *Raion* administration allocated land from this land fund to applicants, bypassing the collective and state farm leadership. The laws also exempted peasant farms from state procurement, exempted peasant farms from land taxes for five years, allowed peasant farms to use hired labor, and provided for unspecified maximum landholding ceilings.

The Communist systems eventual collapse was accelerated in 1985 when President Mikhail Gorbachev set out to reform the system. Realizing the country was near bankruptcy and becoming increasingly isolated from other countries, he sought new ways for generating income and relating to other countries. It was apparent that given the tremendous new developments in technology, travel and communications, Communism could no longer continue in its present form. It was isolated from the rapidly changing world and rapidly depleting its natural and financial resources with little to show for those expenditures outside of its military and space program.

What Gorbachev wanted to do (what he felt he needed to do) was to make the Communist system more efficient, more creative, more modern and more open — and for a while, he was making progress.

However, he forgot one important thing — freedom and control are incompatible. Without tight control, Communism could not survive. And so the more freedom he introduced into the system, the more he lost control — and the more he lost control the more difficult it became for him to preserve the Communist system.

His plans began to unravel in a rather dramatic way in 1989 and 1990, when he lost his Eastern European allies as the Communist systems in those countries collapsed like dominos, almost overnight. The forces he had unleashed at home began to vigorously exercise their new freedoms with a number of demands, i.e., they wanted an end to the Communist Party's monopoly on power; they wanted sovereignty for some of the Republics and full independence for others; and finally, they wanted a radical reform of the economic system and a broader distribution of their national resources and annual output, 50% of which, up until then, was being directed to military and space.

At first, Gorbachev fiercely resisted these demands, and for a while the hard-liners of the Communist Party using the Supreme Soviet as their forum, helped him move to the right of center.

This caused a great deal of unrest in the country, however, and it became very apparent that a reversal in course to the old Communist system was no longer possible without the use of a lot of military force and much bloodshed.

Since Gorbachev had become a world hero for opening up the Communist system, he knew the whole world was watching, and so with his reputation and the future of the Union on the line, he chose not to use force.

Instead, on April 23, 1989 at a location outside of Moscow, Gorbachev organized a quiet, unannounced meeting involving the Council of the Federation, Boris Yeltsin, and eight Republic leaders, and gave in to their demands to essentially dismantle the Soviet Union. This was the last time Gorbachev was really in charge.

In June of 1991, Boris Yeltsin was elected President of the Russian Republic, the Communist Party was declared illegal and the balance of power shifted from Gorbachev and the Soviet Union to Boris Yeltsin and the Russian Republic.

In September the Communist party hard-liners made one more try at turning things around with an attempted coup, but there was little public support and it failed.

On December 8, 1991, Yeltsin met with the leaders of the Ukraine and Byelorussia to declare the formation of a commonwealth of independent states. On Christmas Day, December 25, 1991, Gorbachev resigned and the Soviet Union ceased to exist.

THE AFTERMATH

"In the wake of a democratic revolution, 15 independent states re-emerged from the ruins of the Soviet Union. Yet the overthrow of Communism may be remembered by these nations as child's play, so daunting are the challenges before them.

Politically, they are at risk from within; as Nationalistic demagogues threaten to sabotage the aspiring democracies. Economically, they reel from trial to error, since history offers no guides for the excruciating process of dismantling a long entrenched Communist complex and replacing it with Capitalism."

> National Geographic Society
> Washington, D.C.
> March, 1993

With the overthrow of the Communist system and its economy turned upside down, Russia, and the other newly independent states faced some tough times. There was no financial stability, inflation was rising and there was very little available capital. There were few business laws in place and virtually no one had marketing and financial skills. The former Communist leaders were still in charge but their concept of a democracy, and a market economy, and how to achieve them, was heavily colored by their longstanding beliefs, practices, and experiences in the Communist system.

The old order had been destroyed. Unfortunately, little or no time had been spent in determining what should take its place. There was talk of building a market economy, but little agreement on what that really meant or how it might be established. Younger people for the most part were for it, while older people were generally against it.

To liberals, a market economy meant capitalized markets. To many others, including Gorbachev, it meant a regulated, socialist system. The economy was in shambles and in a frightening tailspin.

This uncertainty and lack of direction generated disrespect for the government and a blatant disregard for government policies. Legal order began to break down and corruption grew. People became increasingly more insecure, more frightened and more aggressive resulting in growing outbreaks of ethnic violence.

7

While democracy was gradually gaining the upper hand over authoritarian Communism, there was no real belief that it would really work. After 74 years under the Communist system, the Russian people lacked initiative, had no orientation to consumerism, and had come to accept poor workmanship as the norm.

Food shortages became a problem of immense proportions. First, because their production per acre was only about half of what it is in the United States; and second, because they lacked the incentives and infrastructure to effectively produce, distribute and market sufficient amounts of high quality food products.

The Western world was happy to see the Communist system collapse but wondered how the wounded Russian "bear" would deal with its problems.

ROBERT SCHULLER OFFERS FOOD AND HOPE

In terms of food, Russia had now come almost full circle to those days following the 1917 Revolution when the Communist Party came into power. Now, like then, Russia's people were in danger of starving and now, like then, an American would play a vital role in supplying them with food.

In 1921 that American was Armand Hammer. In 1991 it was the Reverend Dr. Robert Schuller, famous American tele-evangelist. How these two men came to play those roles is both interesting and ironic.

Armand Hammer's grandparents immigrated from Russia in the late 1800's, before the rise of Communism, and he was to spend a lot of time in Russia beginning soon after the Russian Revolution in 1917.

Born on the lower east side of New York, Hammer made his first million before he was 21. His father turned over the family pharmaceutical business to him while he was attending medical school at Columbia University. Hammer learned quickly how to run the company by day, and study by night. Hammer graduated from medical school and sold the business for a million dollars the same year. He was never to practice medicine, choosing instead, to set "making money" and "helping people" as his goals.

Shortly after graduation in 1921, he heard of the great famine in Russia resulting from the October 17, 1917 Revolution. So flush with cash, Hammer made his first trip to Russia. There the sight of people starving in the streets caused him to offer the Russian government a deal.

The deal was that he would purchase a million dollars worth of grain in the United States and ship it to Russia. In return, Russia would grant Hammer exclusive rights for mining asbestos in their country.

Hammer provided the food he had promised and subsequently made millions from the mining rights he received. Moreover, he forever endeared himself to the Russian people and developed many important friendships in Russia.

Robert Schuller's success story was every bit as dramatic as Armand Hammer's, with two exceptions: where Armand Hammer started out in New York with a million dollars, Dr. Schuller started out on an Iowa farm with nothing; where Armand Hammer's goals were to make money and help people, Robert Schuller's dream was to build a large community ministry for the purpose of introducing Jesus Christ to a multitude of people and helping them to learn about the power and promise of

9

Christianity.

Where Armand Hammer went on to become a billionaire and the Chair of the 16th largest industrial corporation in America, The Occidental Petroleum Company, Dr. Schuller went on to become the most successful and most recognized tele-evangelist minister in the world. Both had a common priority goal: to help people better themselves economically and spiritually. So it was probably pre-ordained that somewhere, somehow their paths would meet and they would collaborate on their common goals.

That time came in 1989 when Hammer, who had made many contributions to the Russian people in his lifetime, felt it was time to present them with another gift, the gift of religious freedom. What gift could be greater for a people who had been forbidden the open existence of religion for over 70 years. The man he would choose to introduce that gift was Robert Schuller.

The choice of Schuller was as appropriate as it was ironic. Fifteen years earlier, on a previous trip to Russia, Schuller had been detained by the KGB, and the Bibles he had brought to Russia had been confiscated.

This time it would be different. Under Gorbachev, things were opening up in Russia and this time Schuller would be in the company of one of Russia's best friends, Armand Hammer.

The goal was to acquire time on Russian television for Schuller's weekly Hour of Power telecast, a program that was already reaching over two million people in the United States and millions more in other countries around the world.

After first spending time with Russia's top leaders, Hammer and Schuller met with Valentin Lazouthkin, head of foreign relations for the Soviet television and radio agency. The conversation went something like this:

> **Hammer**: "I have come here with Dr. Robert Schuller, the most widely respected television pastor in the United States, and I'm asking for your cooperation in letting him put his television program 'Hour of Power' on your network."
>
> **Lazouthkin**: "I am honored you came to see me and I am honored to meet your guest, Dr. Schuller. I'm sure we can come to some kind of an agreement, Dr. Hammer."[4]

---

[4] From the Life of Robert Schuller, James Penner, Author, New Hope Publishing Company, Anaheim, CA, 1992

Schuller's dream, to present God's word in Russia became a reality in 1989 when on Christmas day a special message he taped in Russia was telecast to over 200 million Russian people on channel one, the largest state owned television station in Russia. With that telecast Schuller launched his "Hour of Power" weekly television program on Russian television where it continues today.

From the beginning, until her death in 1998, the telecasts were funded through a generous contribution from Naomi Wilden, a wonderful, humble, Christian woman and philanthropist from Yucaipa, California.

Hammer opened the door, Schuller provided the message and Wilden paid for its showing.

In 1991, recognizing tremendous food shortages as Armand Hammer did in 1921, Dr. Schuller enlisted the aid of World Vision International and Churches Uniting In Global Mission (CUGM), an interdenominational organization of churches which he had just founded, and sent tons of emergency food supplies to Russia where the Russian Orthodox Church distributed them to needy people.

It was this act of kindness and his presence on Russian television which prompted the Supreme Soviet, the upper body of Russia's Parliament, to invite Dr. Schuller to discuss his humanitarian efforts in Russia. During that discussion they asked Dr. Schuller for his assistance in making their agricultural industry more productive. They even offered him land which he could farm. Schuller declined their offer of land and offered instead to find ways for them to make their agriculture more efficient and productive, and while, at the time, he wasn't quite sure how that assistance might be forthcoming, he was sure it would involve Churches Uniting in Global Mission (CUGM), which he had organized early in 1991.

11

PART II

ANSWERING THE CALL

1991-1992

CHURCHES UNITING IN GLOBAL MISSION (CUGM)

Upon his return to the United States, Dr. Schuller told the leadership of Churches Uniting in Global Mission about the request he had received from members of the Duma, and asked them to prepare a response.

Needless to say, this was a bit overwhelming for a group that was still in its infancy. But it also represented a great opportunity to demonstrate their mission "to stand together with our Savior seeking to address the needs of humanity and our environment."

Founded under the leadership of Dr. Schuller, CUGM was established as a network of over 200 pastors from around the world, including the United States, Canada, England, Holland, Russia, and Australia, representing 16 denominations, and many independent churches committed to working together to:

- reach the unchurched
- respond to human needs and the needs of the environment
- restore the image of Christians as people who are positive, honest, compassionate and committed to Christ's mission
- help pastors and their congregations.

At its founding session, church development expert, Lyle Schaller, said of CUGM, "CUGM represents one of the two or three most exciting and innovative approaches to ministry in the new millennium."

One of the initial actions of the founders of CUGM was to elect officers and a General Council which consisted of some of the most prominent and visionary Senior Pastors in America. See Appendix I.

The initial officers of CUGM were Robert Schuller, Chair; Donald Morgan, Senior Pastor, First Church of Christ, Wethersfield, Connecticut, Vice Chair; Robert Lawrence, Senior Pastor, First Congregational Church, Fall River, Maryland, Treasurer; and Thomas E. Reid, Senior Pastor, Full Gospel Tabernacle, Orchard Park, New York, Secretary.

Chester Tolson was chosen to be the Executive Director.

At an organizational meeting of the General Council of CUGM in May, 1991 it was reaffirmed that CUGM was primarily a networking of local congregations across denominational lines throughout the U.S. and the world and its primary aim was "to bring people to Jesus Christ and to his body, the church, utilizing the "Hour of Power" telecast as its voice to connect persons with local congregations in their community."

A number of projects were presented for action including follow-up ministry in areas where the "Hour of Power" telecast is seen and heard; food and clothing to Russia and the other former Soviet Republics, and concerted actions to meet the challenges of America's inner cities.

At this meeting it was also voted by the General Council that a nominated church could become a member of CUGM when the following criteria had been met:

(1) Its senior pastor had attended a CUGM meeting

(2) The General Council had approved the church's request to join CUGM, and

(3) The church paid its annual membership dues of $1,000.00.

This then was the character and purpose of CUGM when Dr. Schuller asked its General Council to prepare a response to the request he received from the members of the Russian Duma.

After some deliberation, the Council accepted the challenge Dr. Schuller had laid before them and asked David Tyler Scoates, Senior Pastor of the Hennepin Avenue Methodist Church in Minneapolis, Minnesota, and a member of CUGM, to organize a task force capable of effectively and meaningfully responding to this unprecedented opportunity to assist the people of Russia in the name of Jesus Christ.

See Appendix I

DAVID TYLER SCOATES
ORGANIZES TASK FORCE

David Tyler Scoates, a powerful speaker and outstanding church leader, took on the task with his usual enthusiasm and determination. There was, of course, some apprehension as well, for the assignment would take him into two areas where he had little direct knowledge and experience - Russia and agriculture.

Nonetheless, as in previous similar situations, he was bolstered by the opportunities he envisioned and the knowledge that he and Dr. Schuller had God and a network of outstanding, highly successful people to assist them.

After much prayer and thought, Scoates assembled a group of dynamic church and business leaders from throughout the United States to discuss the opportunities and challenges encompassed in helping the Russian people to improve their agriculture so they could feed themselves. Included in this group were two persons especially chosen for their agricultural knowledge; Dr. Lee Kolmer, retired Dean of the College of Agriculture, Iowa State University, and Ralph Hofstad, recently retired President and CEO of Land O'Lakes, Inc., a major food and agriculture company with sales of over $2.5 billion annually. Hofstad was also a member of Scoates' Hennepin Avenue Methodist Church.

In September of 1992, Drs. Schuller and Scoates took this group to Russia where they met with members of the Duma, U.S. Ambassador Robert Strauss and Russian agricultural and community representatives to explore how they might develop partnerships and strengthen Russian agriculture and rural communities. Schuller met Mikhail Gorbachev, V.V. Valkov, Boris Yeltsin's, Chief of Staff and leaders of the Russian Orthodox Church during this visit and a subsequent trip to Russia in May of 1993.

The group agreed that whatever they decided to do, their efforts needed to build on and perpetuate new freedoms in Russia: political, religious, economic, and the right to self-determination. Their efforts should be such that they would be sustainable long after their group was no longer involved.

The group also decided that their yet to be determined efforts shouldn't just concentrate on one region in Russia, but serve as a model for the entire country. They felt this was more effective and efficient then trying to do a few things throughout the vast expanse of Russia.

The group visited a number of communities in Russia looking for

16

the "right place" to focus their efforts. Again they had decided the criteria for choosing the "right place":

#1 There needed to be a core of people in the community who were interested and enthused about moving ahead to establish private ownership and individual initiative after the collapse of Communism,

#2 There needed to be local leaders who shared this interest and enthusiasm, and

#3 There needed to be government officials who would provide the support and freedom for people to establish privately-owned farms and businesses.

After visiting a number of areas, the group found those characteristics to be most apparent in the Dmitrov Raion, 70 miles northwest of Moscow, situated in the northeastern part of the Moscow Oblast. This Raion is bordered on the north by Taldon, on the west by Klin and Solnechnnogorsk, on the south by Mytishi and on the east by Sergiev Posad. There are about 251,000 people in the Dmitrov Raion with 70,000 residing in the City of Dmitrov. Dmitrov was founded in 1154 and is situated on the bank of the Yakhroma River in the Volga River Basin. The Dmitrov Raion is one of the leading agricultural areas in the Moscow region specializing in potato, vegetable, and milk production and producing a third of the potatoes and vegetables in the Moscow region.

These agricultural products were being produced by 20 large agricultural joint-stock companies (formerly state and collective farms), 296 individual farms and 22,000 private gardens. Interestingly, 40% of the total potato production, 7.6% of the vegetables and 22.5% of the meat produced in the Dmitrov Raion were being produced by the gardens, which coincidently were permitted to sell their products on the open market when the Communist system was still in operation.

Individual farmers, with an average 7.4 hectares, produced 16.7% of the potatoes and 2.4% of the meat in the Raion. The large joint stock companies, cooperatives, and collective agricultural businesses tended to be highly inefficient and had difficulty sustaining themselves.

The task force decided that CUGM's efforts would focus on four villages: Ramen'ye, Nasadkino, Bunyatino, Gorshkovo, which were once part of one or more state farms.

Having selected the Dmitrov Raion in which to focus their efforts, the next move was to select someone to give day-to-day leadership to the effort. The CUGM leadership needed little time to make that deci-

17

sion. They selected the person in their group who displayed the greatest amount of passion, energy, interest, and enthusiasm for such a project; asked the most questions and offered the most ideas. That person was Ralph Hofstad.

Scoates became chairman of the Project's board of directors and provided outstanding leadership and support until his untimely death in May of 2000.

RALPH HOFSTAD - "COULDN'T BE BETTER"

Since the project I am describing in this book is so completely and inextricably tied to the man CUGM chose to design and lead it, it is important that you know more about him, for without him the project quite probably would never have happened and certainly it wouldn't have had anywhere near the success it has had.

There are many ways to describe Ralph Hofstad, but unfortunately none of them really capture the full essence of this remarkable person.

Born in a Christian home and raised in an urban setting (his father was a Methodist minister) he learned ethics, values and "street smarts" early and has used them as his base throughout his life. He learned about agriculture, farmers, and hard work during summers spent on the farms of relatives in North Dakota and as the president and CEO of some major agricultural cooperatives. He learned to understand and appreciate life in a number of different communities, and even in another country when his father returned the family to Norway, from which he had immigrated, for a two-year period in Ralph's early teens. He learned about business management as an undergraduate at Northwestern University in Illinois and the companies he managed throughout his life.

For 41 years he used what he learned in each of these settings to serve in high level executive positions with major U.S. agribusiness firms, operating as cooperatives, in the upper Midwest. The last 15 of those years he served as President and Chief Executive Officer of Land O'Lakes, Inc., a Fortune 500 agribusiness cooperative with annual sales of $2.5 billion owned by farmers and local cooperatives in 15 states.

The end result is a person with outstanding business sense, a deep appreciation for hard work and integrity and a great compassion for farmers, for agriculture and for the consumers who purchase agricultural products.

But there's so much more that drives and defines Hofstad. First off, he's a visionary who hardly ever chooses to see things as they are but rather wonders what might be if one were creative and willing to expend the resources and effort to effect a change.

He's a risk taker who knows that nothing happens if you don't try. So he tries, knowing that sooner or later he might fail, but even then the learning experience is worth the effort.

He's the most positive person I have ever met, always looking for the proverbial "pony in the manure pile," finding some positive nuggets in almost every situation and usually responding, *"Couldn't have been better"* when asked about meetings, actions or situations.

He's a mentor and a networker who believes deeply in people and their ability to help themselves if they are given the proper support and guidance, and he has a huge network of people to whom he reaches out on a regular basis.

Add to this a seemingly unending amount of energy and enthusiasm which permits him to continue to keep going long after "mere mortals" of half his age, or younger, are left reeling from the pace.

Emerson noted that "nothing great was ever achieved without enthusiasm" so it's not surprising that Ralph Hofstad, who has achieved so much, possesses not only seemingly unlimited and irrepressible enthusiasm but the endurance and determination to overcome major problems and setbacks as well.

Having said all that, it needs to be noted that he is not "pollyannaish." Given all his optimism, energy and enthusiasm, he has retained his ability to think clearly and realistically. He's just not easily dissuaded.

Finally, he is very generous - giving graciously of himself and his financial resources without thought of compensation or recognition, firmly believing that the opportunity to make a difference is compensation and recognition enough.

When he retired from Land O'Lakes in 1989 Hofstad's parting words were "I didn't retire, I graduated! I look forward to at least two new careers; quality time with my family and sharing my 41 years of business experience with those who wish to improve themselves and their communities. I have been richly blessed and I feel compelled to show and give thanks for all the wonderful opportunities that have been afforded me."

This then was the person that Dr. Schuller, Reverend Scoates, and CUGM chose to lead the development effort in Russia and they couldn't have made a better choice. Nor could Hofstad have been more elated. After years of helping people to become more successful and financially secure in the United States, he could now continue such efforts in Russia.

Hofstad's first responsibility, as he saw it, was to find someone in Russia who shared his enthusiasm and energy for helping the Russian people to effectively make the transition from the Communist system to the Private Enterprise System.

Such a person must not only be intelligent, knowledgeable, enthusiastic and energetic, he or she needed to be bilingual, and young enough to see a future for themselves in the new Russia.

Hofstad found that person in Andrei Danilenko, who was in charge of Dr. Schuller's Hour of Power television series in Russia.

> "In my career I have been around a lot of exceptional leaders, but Ralph Hofstad would have to be one of my all time heros with his endless drive, enthusiasm and energy of a 40 year old."
>
> Allen Vangelos
> Former CEO of Calavo
> and RFCP Mentor

> "Ralph Hofstad is truly a master of objective. He combines vision, objectivity and passion in cultivating not only ideas but people. His tears are infectious and his modesty and willingness to learn, humbling. Ralph is one of a few who have changed the course of my life."
>
> Richard C. Watts
> Richard C. Watts Law Firm
> and member of RFCP Board

ANDREI DANILENKO -
NEW GENERATION RUSSIAN

Andrei Danilenko was a perfect match for Hofstad. Not only did he match Hofstad in energy and enthusiasm, he shared his traits as a risk taker and visionary.

Beyond that he was highly intelligent, eager to learn, confident, knowledgeable about the inner workings of Russia and America, and well-connected with key people in Moscow.

Only 28 years of age at the time, he spoke Russian and English fluently (without a hint of an accent) and had already decided that if Russia was to successfully make the transition from Communism to Capitalism, it would be up to his generation to make it happen. Like other young Russians, he felt that the former members of the Communist Party, who were providing the initial leadership in the transition, were too indoctrinated with Communist principles to effectively do the job and the older Russians would not be able to muster the enthusiasm, energy and ideas to carry the banner. Besides, their years of being controlled and repressed by the Communist system had robbed them of the initiative, creativity, and dedication necessary to lead a successful transition.

So, in the minds of Andrei Danilenko and his generation, responsibility for building a new Russia fell to them. Naturally, Danilenko was ready, willing, and eager when Hofstad asked him to get involved in helping the Russian people to improve and restructure their agriculture and their rural communities.

Working with Americans wasn't new to Danilenko. Indeed his mother (an American and a descendant of Germans who once lived in Russia) met his Russian father in Moscow after an international peace conference in Helsinki in 1965. They married in 1969 and lived in Russia from 1969 to 1986, during which time Andrei and his brother Gregory were born. Andrei's father was a professor of Philosophy specializing in Christian Theology at the Moscow Technical College in Moscow.

His parents divorced in 1986 and his mother returned to the United States where she is now on the anthropology faculty at the University of California in Irvine, California. His father became co-owner of a wholesale plumbing supply business.

Andrei keeps in close contact with both. Andrei attended high school in Russia, graduating in 1984. He received his Masters Degree at Moscow State University in 1995.

In 1985 Andrei left Russia to go to the United States to live with his grandmother because he couldn't see any future for himself in Russia under Communism.

In 1989, seeing things beginning to change in Russia, Andrei returned to Russia and made a decision which would set the direction for the rest of his life. He decided he would make his future in Russia, notwithstanding some more immediate rather lucrative opportunities in the United States.

The visionary part of him felt that Russia offered great opportunities for people of his generation if they were willing to work hard, work creatively, take risks and be patient.

The risk taking part of his nature challenged him to go for it. In 1991 he established a center for recovering alcoholics and drug users in Moscow. In 1992 he assumed leadership responsibility for Dr. Schuller's Hour of Power telecasts on a part-time basis. In 1993 that became a full-time position in addition to his responsibilities with RFCP.

His decision to live his life as a Russian was further solidified in 1995 when he took two other major personal steps. He married Zhanna Iuanova, a Russian elementary school teacher, and he joined the Russian Orthodox Church.

With the addition of Danilenko, the project leadership was in place. It was now time to assemble the rest of the team and proceed with the Project.

It was the fall of 1992, 13 months after the collapse of the Communist party.

THE WOMEN FROM OHIO

In addition to Hofstad and Danilenko, two women from Akron, Ohio also played a significant role in the development and establishment of the "Russian project." They are Beth Godard, a businesswoman and member of the founding family of Frito-Lay, and Susan Dudas, Beth's daughter, also an Ohio businesswoman.

When their church pastor, Gabe Campbell, a member of Churches Uniting in Global Mission, was unable to accompany Drs. Schuller and Scoates on their exploratory trip to Russia in 1992, he asked Beth and Susan to represent him on the tour. They went and saw and heard the Russian's plea for help and hope. Deeply moved, they became two of the Project's staunchist early supporters -- giving generously of their resources, expertise, energy and enthusiasm, particularly in matters relating to women and the Russian community. Their efforts will be recounted later in this book. Susan served on the RFCP board from 1995 to 1998 and as one of its most productive mentors.

Beth, also a former board member, now serves as a Trustee Emeritus.

PART III

PREPARING THE RESPONSE

1992-1993

ASSEMBLING THE TEAM

The American Team

With Danilenko aboard, Hofstad set about assembling a team of outstanding American agriculturalists using the network he had so carefully developed and nurtured during his 41-year agribusiness career. Some in his network were former staff members at Land O'Lakes, or at previous companies, others were colleagues, and still others were friends from the business and academic world. He offered them the opportunity to work hard and long, with little or no renmuneration or recognition to help people in rural Russia achieve their dreams for agriculture and their rural communities just like rural Americans did at the turn of the last century. The primary compensation he offered was the opportunity to be a part of an exciting endeavor that would bring hope, opportunity, and success to thousands of people who had suffered under the oppression of Communism. The American team included:

Dr. J.T. Scott, Professor of Agricultural Economics and Director of International Agricultural Programs, Iowa State University, Ames, Iowa, who at the time was serving as a visiting professor at the University of Moscow's internationally renowned Timiryazev Agricultural Academy. J.T. brought invaluable Russian contacts and insights to the initial planning process. He crafted a working relationship between the Academy and the Project and gave leadership to a series of agricultural demonstrations when the Project's initial plans were evolving. He continues as one of it's most productive mentors, making one or two trips to the project site annually.

Dr. Lee Kolmer, retired Dean of the College of Agriculture, Iowa State University, and a person whom Hofstad had invited to accompany the initial task force assembled by Schuller and Scoates in the early explorative state of the project. Kolmer, a rough hewn, outspoken, and respected agricultural academician, played a critically important role in the initial planning phases for the Project; the establishment of a trust fund in Russia; demonstration plots; and crop and livestock production and management courses.

Vern Moore, an agricultural graduate from Iowa State University in Ames, Iowa and long-time associate of Hofstad's at Land O'Lakes and prior cooperatives, was recruited to handle the administrative responsibilities — a role he had handled with great success in his former associations with Hofstad. Moore has few peers in his ability to get a program administratively up and running and assuring its smooth operation once it is launched. People like Moore make it possible for chief executives, like Hofstad, to move ahead in many directions simultaneously knowing that all administrative details related thereto will be handled in a timely and efficient manner.

Susan Dudas, an outstanding young entrepreneur from Akron, Ohio, who was mentioned earlier, joined the team as its first fund raiser. Later she became its human resources specialist and finally the director of the community development portion of the Project. A highly successful, creative and productive person, she brought ideas, enthusiasm and a willingness to roll up her sleeves and get things done. It was Susan who was the mover and shaker behind the dental office which was established by the Project in Ramen'ye, one of the villages in the Dmitrov Raion. It was Susan and her husband, David, who organized and twice lead the TUG program (Teens Uniting Globally) for the Project. More about her later.

Dr. William F. Hueg, retired Vice President for Agriculture, Forestry and Home Economics at the University of Minnesota. A native of Long Island, New York, a graduate of Cornell and Michigan State Universities, and an outstanding agricultural administrator. He and his wife, Hella, established one of the premier dairy herds in Wisconsin following his retirement from the University. He provided advice and assistance in the early phases of the project especially related to dairy farming, management and production.

Larry Becker, a friend of Susan Dudas and Beth Godard from Akron, Ohio, and a graduate of Kent State University, joined the team for a few years as a volunteer private fund raiser, his full-time occupation, when Susan shifted her attention to community development initiatives. Larry brought boundless enthusiasm and creativity to the team in an area where both would be very important.

Ron Hofstad, Ralph's son, gave up his position as Controller at a mainframe computer systems company to become the Project Controller. Ron is a graduate of Iowa State University with a degree in accounting and the University of St. Thomas where he earned an MBA. Ron brings youth, experience, and highly important financial and accounting skills to the team as well as the ability to relate well with the young specialists on the Russian team.

Dr. LaVern (Vern) Freeh, [the author] - Graduate of North Dakota State and Michigan State Universities, Freeh was invited to become part of the initial team that Schuller and Scoates took to Russia, but declined because his wife was dying of cancer and he wanted to spend

27

his time with her. Following her death in 1993, Freeh joined the team to provide leadership in the areas of planning, communication, development, and funding, particularly government funding. Prior to retirement he had been a tenured professor and administrator at the University of Minnesota for 18 years, and Vice President for Public and International Affairs at Land O'Lakes, Inc. for 12 years, part of which was during Hofstad's tenure as President and C.E.O. Freeh currently has a consulting company called Freeh Enterprises in addition to serving as Director of Development.

Two more people were to join the American team a few years later. They are:

Dr. Dennis Behl, who owned a communications company in Minnesota after having served as public relations director for the internationally renown Guthrie Theatre in Minneapolis for ten years. Behl, a graduate of Kent State University in Ohio, served as a communications consultant for the Project. In that role he coordinated media coverage, produced videos about the Project and a quarterly newsletter. Behl left the team in 1998 to return to the Guthrie Theatre staff.

Andre L. Kravchenko, a native of Belarus where he graduated from the Belarussian Economic University in 1995 with a degree in International Economics. Prior to coming to Minnesota, where he plans to pursue an MBA, Kravchenko worked at the Ministry of Foreign Economic Relationships in Minsk in the credit-investment department as assistant to the department head. An intelligent, motivated young man, Andre represents the younger generation of the eastern block countries who will provide the leadership for their country's progress and success in the future. He currently serves as a business development specialist and coordinator of RFCP's new dairy initiative in Russia.

The Russian Team

While Hofstad was assembling the American team, Danilenko was assembling a similar team in Russia, made up of young people eager to be involved in the privatized efforts and older persons with experience and connections that would be critically important to the success of this venture. The Russian team included one American who was married to a Russian woman. They brought a variety of strengths and skills and shared a common passion to be directly involved in the privatization of Russia.

Those who became a part of the Russian team:

Valerie Kuznetsov, a former physics teacher who had taught in Africa, Valerie also once worked for the USSR's State Committee of People's Education. He has been with the Moscow RFCP office since the beginning, where he coordinates scheduling and logistical planning, directs public relations, health, community and social services programs, executes program directives and serves as an interpreter.

Dr. Victor Storozenko, at the University of Moscow's internationally renowned Timiryazev Agricultural Academy, Dr. Storozenko heads the Department of Agriculture of Foreign Countries. He graduated from the Academy in 1964. He also served as the USSR's Minister Counselor in Denmark for nine years. Through the Fulbright Scholars exchange, he hosted Iowa State University's Dr. J.T. Scott on his faculty for three months in 1992. He has been the agricultural technical director for the project since its founding.

Dr. Yuri Izilov, serves as a professor of dairy and cattle production at the Timiryazev Agricultural Academy, and Director of the RFCP Training and Consulting Center, where he instructs farmers and develops the on-going curriculum for the Center. In 1960 he completed his undergraduate degree and in 1969 finished post-graduate studies at Moscow's Timiryazev Agricultural Academy. He has been on the team since the beginning.

Carl Burch, the only expatriate on the Russian team, Burch was raised on a family farm in Boulder, Colorado, he presently serves as the Senior Financial Analyst. A graduate of Colorado State University's Agricultural Business Management program, Burch earned an advanced degree in International Management from the American Graduate School of International Management in Arizona. He spent two years working as a U.S. Peace Corps volunteer, stationed in Mikhailovka in southern Russia where he established a marketing department for an agricultural manufacturing and tractor repair company. He also served as an advisor for a Russian grain trader. It was there that he met his wife, Ludmilla, who has also served as a member of the Russian team from time to time.

Constantine Kravtsov, has a Masters Degree in Economics and presently is in a PhD program in Economics. He graduated from the Moscow University of Consumer Cooperatives and the faculty of International Economy in 1995. He has had four publications in the University Economics Digest. Before joining RFCP he was with the agricultural enterprise "RATAYI" (Kiev, Ukraine), where he coordinated the economics department and was business-manager in the rail transport department of the ball-bearing unit in one of the biggest plants in Russia. At the present time he is responsible for reviewing investments and loans for the Trust Fund.

Muslim Umiryaev, has both a Masters Degree and PhD in Economics. After graduating from a secondary school in Kazakhstan, with honors, he became a student in the Moscow University of the Consumer Cooperatives and the faculty of the International Economy. He has a Diploma in International Economics. Before joining the Trust Fund he previously worked in a commercial bank (international payment systems) and trading company (financial analyst.) He has several publications on finance and international economy. He serves as the Financial Controller of the Moscow team.

Valentin T. Trofimov, serves as a Project Manager, and supervises and coordinates agricultural projects in the Moscow office. He graduated from the Tomsk Institute of Radio Electronics and later the Diplomatic Academy, where he studied International Economic Relations. He served more than 18 years in the Ministry of Foreign Affairs as advisor on science, technology, and agricultural to Russian Ambassadors to Denmark and Finland.

Vasily Tarasov, serves as the Investment Director and is also in charge of credit and legal matters. He has a Masters Degree in Chemical Engineering (oil and gas.) Prior to joining the team he worked for an alcohol and drug treatment center and for the Crystal Cathedral Ministries, Russia.

Natalia Ivanova, serves as Director of Administration and Human Resources. She has a Masters Degree in Engineering. Previous experience includes factory work as a production design engineer. She has had additional training in Human Resources.

Alexander Vinograd, presently serves as Deputy Project Manager. He has a Law Degree and has worked in several foreign countries serving his government in the areas of exports and imports.

Ludmila Tarasova, served as the Chief Accountant for RFCP and is now the Internal Auditor. She has a degree in Economics and has done planning and development work in a heavy industry research institute in Russia.

Kuznetsov, Storozenko, Izilov, and Burch were members of the original team. The others joined later.

THE BOARD OF DIRECTORS

In its formative years, the General Council of Churches Uniting in Global Mission (CUGM) served as the Board for the Russian Farm Community Project (RFCP).

They were replaced by RFCP's own board when RFCP became an independent 501 3c (non-profit) organization in 1995. Some of the CUGM General Council members became members of the RFCP board at that time.

Much of RFCP's success through the years can be attributed to the guidance and support it has received from its board.

The board is made up of an outstanding group of people representing a broad cross section of skills, experiences and geographic locations. They include business executives, a banker, farmers, a lawyer, a former university president and administrator of the U.S. Agency for International Development, and four clergy.

All are outstanding leaders who have achieved notable success in their lives. All are passionately dedicated to the mission and goals of RFCP and have given generously of themselves and their resources.

The first Chair of the Board was David Tyler Scoates. When he joined the CUGM staff as its Executive Director in 1994, Dr. Otis Young, Senior Minister of First Plymouth Congregational Church in Lincoln, Nebraska became Chair. He still serves in that position.

RFCP BOARD MEMBERS

Dr. Otis Young - Senior Minister, First Plymouth Congregational Church, Lincoln, Nebraska. Appointed by Presidents Reagan and Bush to serve on the U.S. Advisory Council for Voluntary Foreign Assistance, USAID. Dr. Young advised the U.S. State Department on the disbursement of foreign assistance to countries around the world. A civic leader and pastor of one of Nebraska's largest congregations, he is recognized as a champion of humanitarianism. He chairs the RFCP Board of Directors (since 1994) and recently led the Board to a special meeting with the Russian Ambassador at the Embassy of the Russian Federation in Washington, D.C. He is a Trustee of Doane College, the Bryan Memorial Hospital and the President's Advisory Board of the University of Nebraska.

Dr. Ronald Roskens - CEO, Global Connections, Inc., Omaha, Nebraska. Roskens become president of Global Connections, Inc., an international business consulting firm, in 1996. He was previously associated with the InterAction Council, a group of 35 former heads of State or Government. Prior to these assignments, Roskens served as Administrator, U.S. Agency for International Development (USAID), a position to which he was appointed to by President Bush. In this position, he was the chief executive officer of a $7.5 billion program of economic and humanitarian assistance to more than 100 countries in the developing world. Prior to this appointment, he had over 30 years of service in administration, teaching and research that began as a professor at Kent State University and culminated in his appointment as president of the University of Nebraska system.

Richard C. Watts - Attorney, Santa Ana, California. A practicing attorney, he has served as International Director of the Robert Schuller Ministries and is active with several non-profit youth programs in Orange and Los Angeles counties, including the Orange County YMCA. He visited Russia in 1997, and was instrumental in RFCP receiving a bankrupt processing facility from the Mayor of Moscow.

Dr. Norman Broadbent - Senior Minister, Falcon Heights United Church of Christ. He hold degrees from Drury College (MO), Pacific School of Religion - Berkeley and the School of Theology at Claremont (CA). He has had active community leadership roles which coincided with his local church pastorates, as well as leadership positions within the structure of his denomination. He provides the leadership for RFCP's Youth Initiatives such as TUG, TUGR, and YAARN.

Larry Buegler - Served as Director of Planning and Economic Development and Executive Director of its Housing and Redevelopment Authority in St. Paul, Minnesota. Before that, he was Chief of Party, for a large agricultural credit program in Russia. He was also President and CEO of the Farm Credit Bank of St. Paul and Norwest Bank, St. Paul. He has degrees in Law (William Mitchell College of Law) and Economics (University of Minnesota.)

Alona Vrieze -Born and raised in Novosibirsk, Siberia, she received her education in International Studies at the University of Novosibirsk. She has also lived in the Czech Republic as a representative of american businesses. She has a Masters Degree in finance from the University of St. Thomas, St. Paul, MN, and is a partner with her husband in a commercial dairy farm. She serves as Secretary for the RFCP Board of Directors.

Priscilla Felisky Whitehead - Minister, The Church by the Sea, Bal Harbour, Florida. She has family ties in Russia, and is a frequent visitor there. She speaks Russian and brings and understanding of Russian culture to the Board.

Dr. Gordon Powell - Senior Minister, North Main Street Church of God, Butler, Pennsylvania. He has long history with this church, and has helped develop well-organized social outreach programs there. Has made two trips to the RFCP location in Russia. Is one of the original RFCP Directors.

John Cotton - Serves as a farm manager for a large number of farms in Iowa, Minnesota, and South Dakota. A graduate of Iowa State University, he has used his farm management training to become one of the most successful managers in his field. He also serves on many boards and committees, and is known for his financial development expertise.

John Vrieze - Born and raised in Baldwin, Wisconsin and has lived on a farm all of his life. After attending college at the University of

Wisconsin, River Falls, he returned to the farm and entered the dairy business. His present herd size is 2,400 dairy cows. In addition, he sells Registered Holstein embryos to nine foreign countries and commercial dairy cows to 29 states as well as to Canada and Mexico. Vrieze provides overall leadership for RFCPs dairy initiatives.

Emeritus Directors:

Dr. Lee Kolmer - Dean of Agriculture (retired), Iowa State University. Has a long history of international development work while in the university system. Was one of the original RFCP directors, and has made many trips to the RFCP in Russia. Serves as Technical Director for RFCP.

Betty Godard, Akron, Ohio - Semi-retired business woman and homemaker. With her daughter, Susan Dudas, is one of the founders of RFCP. Has made several trips to the project site in Russia. She operated an automobile agency with her son after the death of her husband. Is very active in local church and civic organizations.

PAST BOARD MEMBERS

Dr. David Tyler Scoates - (Deceased) Past President of Robert Schuller Ministries and Pastor, Crystal Cathedral, Garden Grove, California. Dr. Scoates was appointed by Dr. Schuller in 1992 to respond to a request from Russian Parliament leaders to assist their agricultural community to produce enough food to feed their country. In the winter of 1991-92, much food and clothing had been sent by U.S. churches to respond to the great need at that time. In response to this follow-on request, Dr. Scoates, with the assistance of Ralph Hofstad, led a team of business, university, and church leaders to Russia to study the situation. On his return, he provided the initial direction and leadership for RFCP and became the first Chair of the Board.

Susan Dudas - Akron, Ohio, Founder and principal consultant of the Russel Group, specialized in human resources and career consulting for a number of years. She holds a Master's Degree in human resources. Dudas also owned a manufacturing company, New Era Transportation, Inc. and was honored with the SME Distinguished Sales and Marketing Award for her efforts and outstanding results at New Era Transportation. Currently she and her husband operate a charter school in Akron, Ohio. She is the Chief Architect of RFCP's Community and Youth Initiatives.

Gerald Meigs - St. Paul, Minnesota, Vice President and Shareholder of St. Paul Book and Stationary Company for 34 years; former District Governor of Rotary and currently on the Rotary International Foundation Board

William Cornhoff - Chagrin, Ohio, Works with high net individuals, corporations, trusts and non-profit entities in designing, implementing, and monitoring investment strategies to meet their respective goals and objectives. His product knowledge includes stocks, government and corporate bonds, municipal bond, options and mutual funds.

Walter Siemens - Trail, British Columbia, Canada, Owner and CEO of a major insurance company; his parents immigrated from Ukraine; and he and his wife were on 1996 tour to Russia.

Wayne Yeager - Louisville, Kentucky, Senior minister, St. Mark's

Episcopal Church, Louisville, Kentucky. One of the original RFCP directors, he has made two trips to the RFCP in Russia. He serves one of the leading church congregations in Louisville, which has active programs for all groups in society.

See Appendix II

CHARTING THE COURSE

With the project location identified and the team in place, what followed were a series of staff and board meetings in California, Minnesota, and Russia during which the Project gained a title, "The Russian Farm Community Project" (RFCP.) Its offices were established in Minneapolis and Moscow; and the following mission, objectives, and guiding principles for RFCP were finalized and recorded:

The Mission

The Russian Farm Community Project exists for the sole purpose of assisting people in designated rural communities of Russia to effectively make the transition from a centrally planned food and agricultural system to a market driven system.

Some of the choices they will need to make in the process will require taking risks from which they were shielded under the Communist system.

The Objectives
1. Help rural Russian people to achieve a better quality of life through the use of improved agricultural practices and the development of a more efficient food and agricultural system and infrastructure.
2. Help rural Russian people to privatize profitable operations individually or collectively and create new jobs.
3. Provide U.S. technical advisors to help the Russian people to adopt newer technologies and practices for their food and agricultural system and their rural communities.
4. Secure funds and provide capital in the form of loans and equity investments for the establishment of private farms and businesses and critically needed infrastructure.
5. Establish a Russian Trust Fund which will serve as a vehicle for receiving, managing and dispersing project funds to ventures which are based on sound business practices.
6. Identify local leaders and provide them with encouragement, training and support whenever possible.
7. Help the rural people to improve and reconstruct their social programs and generally improve the quality of their community life by assisting them in the establishment of:
    -   Readily accessible health care at affordable prices,

38

- Computer and English classes,
- Adequate and affordable housing, and
- Youth Programs.

8. Establish the Russian Farm Community Project's efforts as a model from which other communities can learn.

Guiding Principles

Ventures supported and funded by the Russian Farm Community project (RFCP) must:

- Be led by Russians,
- Respect Russian culture,
- Offer choices to the Russian people, and
- Utilize appropriate technology and sound business practices.

WHY RUSSIA? WHY AGRICULTURE?

During the process of defining the mission and objectives of the Russian Farm Community Project, two questions often arose. In America people asked, "Why would you want to help the Russians?" In Russia people wondered why Americans would leave their comfortable homes, travel half way around the world, and often live in less than desirable conditions, to help people who were once considered their enemies. In America the question was much the same.

Why Russia?

Why help Russia? RFCP's answer quite simply was and is, "Because they need us and over the long haul, we and our children will need them as well."

While that may be reason enough for some people, there are other more compelling reasons as well. The first relates to world peace and stability, neither of which can be assured if the Russians are unsuccessful in their quest for freedom, democratic governance, economic growth, and reform.

The second major reason is to create new and expanding opportunities for American and Russian businesses, large and small, to participate in Russias newly emerging marketplace.

Like it or not, everyone (Russian and American) has a stake in what happens in Russia over the next decade. By seizing this rare opportunity to "help" rather than "hate" the Russians, and linking our economies and our expertise with theirs, Americans can provide much needed assistance and prosper from the more stable global community which they help to create.

Why Agriculture?

Again, the answer was and is simply - because agriculture is Russia's area of greatest need.

Following the collapse of Communism, the agricultural sector was largely forgotten in the rush to develop Russia's urban areas. The consequence, was and is, a farm to food system which is in critical need of repair, support and direction and rural people who are struggling to survive while many of their urban counterparts are reaping the benefits of economic freedom. The possibility of severe food shortages, and a continued inability to meet basic needs in rural areas, threaten the fragile framework of democratization, economic and political reform and the demilitarization now taking place in Russia, the Ukraine and other former Republics.

Andre Danilenko was quite emphatic, when he said on a number of occasions, "My nation cannot feed its own people. Today over 65% of our food is imported."

> "My nation...cannot feed its own people. Today 65% of our food is imported. This must change."
>
> - - Andrei Danilenko

DECIDING WHERE TO BEGIN

The next step in the planning process was somewhat akin to deciding where to begin hugging an elephant. The task seemed so huge, the needs of the Russian people so immense and the opportunities and potential problems almost beyond comprehension.

Fortunately, or unfortunately, depending on ones perspective, most of the U.S. staff and many of the Russian staff had spent much of their lives in an environment of challenge, helping people convert problems into opportunities.

Those who hadn't had such experiences were swept along by the energy and enthusiasm of Hofstad, Danilenko, and the others who had.

After numerous staff meetings it was decided that five things would be necessary for the project to be successful:

#1   The Russian Farm Community Project would need the support and assistance of the Russian Government (the Dmitrov Raion) and the U.S. Government.

#2   There needed to be a way to immediately demonstrate to the Russians that the Americans were serious in their intention to help the Russian people and that those efforts would be meaningful.

#3   There needed to be a rather large pool of funds available to finance the Project, and a financial structure and system for receiving, and effectively managing and dispersing these funds.

#4   There needed to be a facility, equipment, course materials, and instructors for teaching those who would receive loans from RFCP about the rudiments of the free enterprise system. Courses needed to be offered on such topics as credit, profit, management, business plans, etc., all of which are critically important in a private enterprise system. Finally,

#5   Opportunities and assistance must be made available to both those who were interested in establishing their own farms and businesses and former state and collective farms that wished to become more efficient and productive.

Looking at the list, Hofstad stated, "Our cup runneth over, so let's get started." To which Danilenko added, "One thing is certain, we will be working in the two highest risk segments of the Soviet economy, rural Russia and agriculture."

> "We will be working in two of the highest risk segments of the Soviet economy, rural Russia and agriculture."
>
> - - Andrei Danilenko

PART IV

SETTING THE STAGE/THE EARLY YEARS

1992-1994

PROLOGUE

With the preliminary planning completed, RFCP now set its sights on implementation and the building of the foundation on which its initiatives would be built.

Partnerships needed to be established, plans needed to be finalized and the cornerstones for a successful economic development model needed to be put into place.

This section tells how it was done.

PARTNERING WITH THE RUSSIAN PEOPLE

Most of RFCP's early efforts in Russia were focused on meeting with people in rural areas to determine their needs and their wants, their problems and their concerns, their hopes and their dreams. Trying to ascertain what they were willing and capable of accomplishing, trying to understand and quantify the impediments they faced and what it would take to remove those impediments, trying to find those who would be willing to go the extra mile and work that extra hour to succeed, trying to find ways to motivate them to take ownership for their future.

While the Russian people were generally quite excited about the prospect of partnering with RFCP and eagerly participated in the early meetings with Hofstad, Danilenko and the others, they were also somewhat apprehensive.

They had no experience and little or no knowledge about such things as democracy and the free enterprise system.

They had spent their lives in a culture, where on the surface people seemed to favor strong centralized government control (what choice did they have?), but in actuality spent a great deal of their time figuring out creative ways to work around that control.

They had learned to avoid writing things down or to leave "paper trails" that could be used against them by central government, especially at tax time.

They had become quite creative in their use of barter and the black market "the underground market."

Most tried to avoid rising too far above their peers in terms of material possessions so as not to be ostracized in a culture that frowned on anyone "getting too far ahead of the crowd."

During the course of these early meetings, the people Hofstad, Danilenko, and their staffs were seeking began to emerge. People who had an entrepreneurial spirit; people who were willing to learn about the private enterprise system and what it took to succeed in such a system; people who wanted to take advantage of their new found freedoms and build a better life for themselves and their children. Some of them are profiled later in this book.

It was with these people, at the local level, that RFCP formed a partnership that was to be the foundation of its efforts. Most were in their 30s or early 40s.

It was these people who helped finalize the concept for RFCP's efforts i.e.

1. RFCP's clients would be comprised of three types of people:
   - Homesteaders and Entrepreneurs,
   - Privatized family farmers, and
   - Privatized collective farmers.
2. The initial area served would be the Dmitrov Raion and the villages of Ramenýe, Bunyatino and Nasadkino.
3. The goal would be to serve the agricultural and business needs of these areas, assisting the people to establish profitable farming and business operations.
4. Loans and credit services, educational courses and demonstrations, technological assistance and mentoring programs would be the manner in which this assistance would be provided.
5. A trust fund, a training and education center, and a business development center would also be established to provide these services and programs.

With the partnership defined, the next step was to build partnerships with others who would be critically important to the success of RFCP's initiatives i.e. the local administrator (government entity) a major Russian University; the U.S. Government and any others that were interested and could assist.

PARTNERING WITH THE RUSSIAN GOVERNMENT

Even before the breakup of the Soviet Union in August 1991, power over the agrarian reform was being transferred to the republic level. This included responsibility for social services, which were formerly provided by the collective and state farms.

One of the most significant legal developments in Russia's agrarian reform occurred in November 1992, when the Russian Supreme Soviet enacted a law providing that those who held small plots of land would have full ownership, with the right to buy and sell such plots in direct transactions with other individuals. Then, in December, the Russian Congress of Peoples' Deputies amended the Russian Constitution to give holders of small land plots full ownership rights, including the right to buy and sell land directly to other individuals. These two enactments allowed those who held private plots on former or present collective and state farms, (garden plots, and *dacha* plots or country cottages) to buy and sell such plots.

One of the local government's first actions was to authorize penalties for farm managers who obstructed would-be-peasant farmers from receiving the land due them under their share.

In terms of full-size farms, the constitutional amendment allowed private sale to individuals only after ten years for land that was received free, and after five years for land that was purchased. In the interim, such land could be sold only to the local government.

The transfer of power to the local administration was good news for the Russian Farm Community Project because it meant that they could deal directly with the administration of the Dmitrov Raion on matters relating to policies, land ownership, and government assistance, thereby, bypassing the huge and cumbersome national government system. Moreover, the initial CUGM/RFCP exploratory group had chosen the Dmitrov Raion because they felt its administration would be supportive and helpful.

In the spring of 1993 Hofstad and Danilenko visited the office of V.V. Gavrilov, Head of Administration for the Dmitrov Raion (also referred to as Governor in other parts of this book), to inform him of their ideas and invite him to be part of RFCP's plans for the future. He welcomed them with open arms and assured them he wanted to be part of their efforts.

Gavrilov, an energetic, popular and highly competent new generation Russian in his mid-forties, had been involved in the Raions administration since 1987, having served as Vice Mayor and Mayor of Dmitrov before being appointed Head of Administration for the Dmitrov Raion in 1991, a position to which he was elected by a 90% majority in 1993.

Like Hofstad and Danilenko, Gavrilov is a visionary and a doer. Moreover, he was enthused about the presence of the Russian Farm Community Project in his Raion and eager to do what he could to support RFCP's efforts. He would prove to be a most outstanding ally.

"I trust you" were his words to Hofstad as he signed a Memorandum of Agreement on September 30, 1993, in which he agreed to provide support and assistance to RFCP's projects in Dmitrov and provide 5,000 acres of land under his jurisdiction to be used for "homesteading" up to 25 farm families on their own farms over the "next five years."

> "I trust you that is why I am pleased to sign this agreement with you."
>
> V.V. Gavrilov
> Head of Administration
> Dmitrov Raion

See Appendix III

50

PARTNERING WITH A RUSSIAN UNIVERSITY

Having established the base for a working relationship with the people and the administration of the Dmitrov Raion, Hofstad and Danilenko next turned their attention to finding an educational institution and faculty in Russia that might be interested in being a part of RFCP's efforts in Dmitrov.

Their search for a Russian university partner was driven by three primary reasons:

#1 Hofstad knew how important U.S. Land Grant Universities had been in the development of agriculture and rural communities in the United States through their education, research and extension programs,

#2 Both Hofstad and Danilenko felt they needed to tap into the expertise and knowledge relating to Russian agriculture and its rural communities, which was present in Russian academic institutions specializing in agriculture, and

#3 They felt that a Russian agricultural academic institution could provide expertise and assistance for developing demonstration plots and agricultural courses and assist in the establishment and operation of a field headquarters and an educational and training center in the Dmitrov Raion.

They found the academic institution they were looking for in the Timiryazev Agricultural Academy (TAA) in Moscow and strong faculty interest in persons like Victor Storozhenko, specialist in agronomy and Yuri Izilov, specialist in dairy.

Primary credit for leading Hofstad and Danilenko to the Timiryazev Agricultural Academy (TAA) goes to Dr. J.T. Scott of Iowa State University who was a visiting professor at the academy at the time, under a Fulbright Scholarship.

Timiryazev Agricultural Academy (TAA)

Timiryazev Agricultural Academy was established approximately a century ago. Its structure includes three levels of administration:

51

(1) divisions, (2) departments, and (3) organization-wide central administration headed by the Rector with two or three assistants called Prorectors.

The divisions include, but are not limited to, the areas of: Plant Sciences, Animal Sciences, and Social Sciences. Departments are many and varied including world agriculture, farm management, cybernetics, dairy science, horses, and poultry, to name a few. Originally the academies were specialized teaching institutions. Presently they consider themselves as both research and teaching institutions enrolling graduate students as well as undergraduates. Extension programs (as we know them) had not existed prior to 1990.

The Academy is located in Moscow. This proximity to central government agencies provides the Academy with many contacts and consultancies with governmental employees and officers. It also gives TAA access to funding opportunities and recognition as the premier agricultural academy of Russia.

In 1992, RFCP and the Academy entered into a partnership agreement whereby RFCP and TAA would cooperate in facilitating the privatization of Russian agriculture; improving the productivity of Russian farmers; developing an education and training center to provide educational courses and demonstrations, and disseminating current agricultural information on such things as production, management and marketing. They also agreed to assist in seeking funds from foundations, government agencies and international organizations, helping convert an elementary school into a first class training and education center with state-of-the-art equipment; and providing faculty support for U.S. mentors.

The immediate objectives for this RFCP/university partnership were to:
1. Plan and conduct research and demonstration plots and projects in potatoes, vegetables, silage, and seed crops to demonstrate the value of good management, high quality seed and optimum fertilizer and plant production procedures.
2. Establish an agribusiness department and an extension program which would include an undergraduate curriculum in agribusiness and an agricultural management research program.
3. Establish an extension education and training program at the education and training center in Ramenýe and place resident teachers at the facility on a rotating basis to develop and teach courses in farm management, farm accounting, agricultural

marketing, business plan development and credit, with the assistance of U.S. mentors with expertise in these areas.
4. Organize courses and programs to enhance the quality of life in the rural communities of Russia through programs and improvements in the communities' infrastructure, health services, nutrition, education, and social services.

See Appendix IV

DEFINING THE TERMS OF THE PARTNERSHIP

Having established partnerships with the people, the local government and a Russian university, Hofstad and Danilenko moved now to establishing the terms.

The terms which were agreed on by RFCP and its Russian partners identified three areas where immediate assistance was needed: Capital, Technology and Education and Training:

1. In the Area of Capital

RFCP Agreed To:
·   Solicit funds from public and private sources in U.S. and elsewhere.
·   Establish a trust fund in Russia for the disbursement of funds in the form of loans or as equity investments.
·   Assist in identifying, educating and assisting persons and entities requiring loans and equity investment.

The Russian Partners Agreed To:
·   Assist in the establishment and operation of a trust fund.
·   Assist in the development and monitoring of business and financial plans and to do their best to assure the timely payback of loans (with a modest interest fee) to replenish the trust fund.
·   Assist in identifying persons and entrepreneurs who were good risks for loans and investments.

2.   In the Area of Technical Assistance

RFCP Agreed To:
·   Assist in determining the type of technical assistance needed.
·   Acquire and install new and needed technology.
·   Establish a mentoring program for bringing U.S. experts to Russia for varying lengths of time to install and develop understanding of new technology.

The Russian Partners Agreed To:
·   Provide land for homesteading and private farming (government).
·   Identify the type of technical assistance needed.

- Assist in installation and utilization of technology.
- Provide technical experts from Russian universities.
- Leadership and support from local government.
- Agricultural research opportunities and capabilities.

In the Area of Education and Training

RFCP Agreed To:
- Assist in the establishment, equipping and staffing of a training and education center.
- Provide leadership and mentors for the development of demonstrations, courses and materials to teach farmers and those interested in owning their own farms and businesses, the principles of private enterprise and their use in establishing and operating private enterprises.

The Russian Partners Agreed To:
- Identify and support people in Russia who have a desire for private ownership and a willingness to learn and perform.
- Assist RFCP in the establishment and staffing of a training and education center and educational materials, courses, and demonstration relating to the private enterprise system.

BUILDING A TRAINING AND
EDUCATION CENTER

Since education and training were one of the three highest priority needs identified by the Russian partners and RFCP they began immediately to explore ways and means for building a training and education center in the Dmitrov Raion.

Given the distance (70 miles) between RFCP's Russian headquarters in Moscow the Timiryazev Agricultural Academy (also in Moscow) and the Dmitrov Raion, such a center would serve both as RFCP's field headquarters and a place where the participating Russian people could partake of educational short courses and mentoring and extension services related to the free enterprise system. The concept was excellent. Implementation was more difficult.

Having spent their entire lives in a centrally controlled environment where most decisions were made for them, most Russian people have little or no experience or knowledge about such things as business plans, cash flow, credit, profit and loss, and enterprise management.

Moreover, having lived in a culture which has an aversion to written documents (for fear they might later be used against them) the Russian people are, by nature, very reluctant to commit things to paper.

Nevertheless, Hofstad, Danilenko and their Russian partners pressed on toward the establishment of a training and education center in the village of Ramenýe in the Dmitrov Raion.

They knew that without the knowledge and acceptance of basic free enterprise "tools" including written plans and records, the Russians could not succeed in their privatization efforts.

The village of Ramenýe was chosen as the site because it had an underutilized elementary school which had potential for being remodeled into a training and education center.

The first step was to ask the Raion's administrator, Mr. V.V. Gavrilov for permission to convert the elementary school into such a center. Because of his keen interest and involvement in RFCP's plans and efforts and the dwindling numbers of students being served by the facility, he was pleased to do so with two provisions: (1) the costs for remodeling and equipping the center would need to be covered by RFCP, and (2) RFCP would need to be willing to share the building with the elementary students until they could be transferred to another location.

Ironically, the school stood literally in the shadow of St. Mathews Church, a Russian Orthodox Church which for 74 years, during the

Communist regime, had served first as a grainery and later as a recreational center before being returned to its original function as a church following the collapse of Communism.

RFCP acquired private funds for remodeling the elementary school building, a group of U.S. Rotary clubs provided funding for equipping it with state-of-the-art computers and other educational equipment and the Training and Education Center became a reality.

The RFCP staff worked with Professors Viktor Storozhenko and Yuri Izilov of the Timiryazev Agricultural Academy and U.S. advisors in developing educational materials for a series of short courses on business and management at the center. Professor Izilov was appointed director of the center.

Following a ribbon cutting and building dedication ceremony during the summer of 1994, the building was officially opened.

The center serves two primary purposes:

1. It's the area administrative office for the Russian Farm Community Project and provides:
    *   Business and Accounting Services for RFCP initiatives in the area.
    *   Central co-ordinating point for RFCP projects in the area.

2. It's the training and education center for RFCP and provides:
    *   Consulting services and facilities for private farmers, rural communities, cooperatives, entrepreneurs and emerging businesses
    *   Business and Accounting Courses
    *   Office space for visiting U.S. and Russian mentors
    *   Business library and service center for people of the area, including e-mail, copier, and fax services
    *   Storage for project training and administrative materials, equipment and records

Courses offered since the center was established include:
*   Farm Management Practices
*   Asset Management Practices
*   Business Plan Development
*   Credit — its purpose, value and cost
*   Cash Flow

- Profit and Loss - character and measurements
- Record keeping for measuring success

The center serves as a link between the staff of Timiryazev Agricultural Academy, and U.S. mentors and local farmers and entrepreneurs at the grassroots level, addressing local needs through short courses, mentors or farm/business extension specialists "who call on participating area farmers and entrepreneurs" on a regular basis.

The center attracted a lot of attention within Russia and internationally and grew to the point where it needed to be moved to another, larger, more centralized and accessible location in Dmitrov. This was done in 1998.

ESTABLISHING A MENTORING PROGRAM

From the beginning it was obvious to Hofstad and Danilenko that it would be physically and financially impossible to assemble a full time staff that encompassed all of the knowledge, experiences, skills and talents that would be needed to achieve the goals the Russian Farm Community Project had set for itself.

Just as a variety of partnerships needed to be developed with government agencies, educational institutions and development organizations, mentors would need to be recruited who had the interest, abilities, and passion to help RFCP make a difference in Russia.

If Hofstad, Danilenko, their staffs, and the Russian people, were the heart and soul of RFCP's efforts, the mentors would represent the life blood, continually bringing new insights, new talents, skills, and ideas to the Russian people.

Mentors join the RFCP team for varying lengths of time, as needed, to carry out specific assignments and/or deal with pressing needs.

Some are recruited after an extensive search for just the "right person"; some "right persons" are already on the scene and some hear about the project, like what they hear and see, and volunteer to mentor an area that needs mentoring.

Some mentors have became members of the RFCP board. Others served on the staff or board for periods of time.

All who served, or are serving as mentors, have one thing in common, they are talented, successful people who are drawn to RFCP because they see it as a great opportunity to share their knowledge and skills; to live out their passion for helping others; to travel and make new friends, and to make a difference in the lives of those less fortunate then they. Most have served without remuneration other than their expenses.

While their efforts and accomplishments will be noted later in this book it is most appropriate that their names, background, and the areas in which they served as mentors, be recorded in this section as well.

Mentor
   Dr. Lee Kolmer
Background
   · Agricultural Economist and Farm Management Specialist
   · Former Dean, Iowa State University College of Agriculture
   · Member of Initial RFCP Team

Area Mentored
- Demonstration Plots
- Course Development
- Trust Fund
- Farm Management

Mentor
Dr. J.T. Scott
Background
- Agricultural Economist
- Professor of Agricultural Economics and Director of International Agriculture Programs at Iowa State University
- Fulbright visiting professor at Timiryazev Agricultural Academy, Moscow

Area Mentored
- Demonstration Plots
- Course Development
- Strategic Planning

Mentor
Beth Godard
Background
- Businesswoman with a number of significant business ventures in the Akron Ohio area

Area Mentored
- Community initiatives
- Business opportunities for Russian women
- Housing

Mentor
Susan Dudas
Background
- Businesswoman from Akron, Ohio
- Involved in a number of business and educational ventures in the Akron, Ohio area
- Daughter of Beth Godard

Area Mentored
- Community initiatives
- Russian women
- Dental clinic

- Youth initiatives
- Human Resources

Mentor
Brian Foster
Background
- Iowa farmer
- Graduate of Iowa State University
- Served as Director for Volunteers for Overseas Cooperative Assistance (VOCA) in Russia from 1991 to 1994

Area Mentored
- Loan program
- Homesteading program

Mentor
Ray Jilek
Background
- North Dakota businessman

Area Mentored
- Farmers Marketing Association

Mentor
Allen Vangelos
Background
- California business executive
- Former President and CEO of major agricultural cooperative in California

Area Mentored
- Processing, distribution and marketing center

Mentor
John Vrieze
Background
- Outstanding Wisconsin dairy farmer
- Successful in selling dairy cattle embryos to Russia
- Married to a Russian native

Area Mentored
- Farm Supplies and Services
- All phases of a major dairy initiative

Mentor

  Dr. Norman Broadbent

Background

· Pastor of United Church of Christ in Falcon Heights, Minnesota

· Outstanding abilities in youth and community development work

Area Mentored

· Youth and young adult Initiatives

· Community Initiatives

Mentor

  Dr. Norman Westhoff

Background

· Medical doctor from Roseville, Minnesota

· Specialist in Occupational Health

Area Mentored

· Health Initiatives

Mentor

  Doug Aretz

Background

· Social worker from St. Cloud, Minnesota

· Administrator of elderly care center

Area Mentored

· Care and Housing of Elderly Initiatives

Mentor

  Gary Buttermore

Background

· Sawmill operator in Iowa

Area Mentored

· Sawmill

Mentor

  Cheryl Hensley

Background

· Marketing specialist

· Provided by the Citizens Network for Foreign Affairs

Area Mentored

· Marketing Study

Mentor

Bob Clark

Background

- Outstanding career with Countrymark Cooperative in Indiana, Michigan, Ohio
- Excellent record of turning around failing cooperatives
- President and CEO of Cooperative Business International (CBI)

Area Mentored

- Farm Supplies and Services Initiative

PLANTING SEEDS OF HOPE

If a picture is worth a thousand words, as some have said, then a demonstration plot should be worth even more, especially in an environment where the American and Russian participants have no common culture or language to fall back on.

With that in mind, and because RFCP needed to show early on that it was serious in its intent to help the Russian people, a series of demonstration plots were established under the leadership of Drs. J.T. Scott and Lee Kolmer of Iowa State University, and Dr. Victor Storozhenko of the Timiryazev Academy, the first "mentors" associated with RFCP. The purpose of these "test" plots was to show how yields of crops such as potatoes could significantly be increased through the introduction of new variables relating to management: varieties, fertilizer, manure, herbicides, and cultivation methods.

The first demonstration plots were established in the spring of 1993 on a farm owned by the Russian Orthodox Church near Kaluga, and a former collective farm in Dmitrov. The purpose was to test new varieties of potatoes and the value of fertilizer, herbicides and new cultivation methods in increasing yields per hectare. The two locations were chosen because they represented both a northern site and a southern site in the region. A May Day tour of the plots was held for U.S. and Russian persons interested in the Project.

In the fall of 1993 field days were conducted at the demonstration plot sites during which the startling results of the demonstrations were discussed with people from the areas in which the plots were located; i.e, a ten-fold increase in yield at the Kaluga site and a fifty percent increase at the Dmitrov site.

These results really caught the attention of the Russian farmers, and RFCP received many requests from individual farmers and huge state and collective farms (now operating as Joint Stock Companies) to establish demonstration plots on "their" farms the next year.

In the spring of 1994 potato and corn (for silage) demonstration plots were planted in Dmitrov resulting in a 300% increase in yields.

Building on those dramatic results, RFCP offered its first potato production short course to farmers in the fall of 1994.

In subsequent years the demonstration plots were expanded in scope and variety, and established on private farms and joint stock company farms with continuing success.

In the words of Dr. J.T. Scott, "There is nothing quite as persuasive for farmers, whatever the country, as digging down in that soil and coming up with results — a greater number of larger potatoes and other vegetables at harvest time. The proof that new growing methods work is right there in your hand. Lots of Russian private farmers are hungry for that kind of solid, <u>seeing is believing</u>, evidence."

The primary reason for bringing the demonstration plots to private farms was to demonstrate improved methods directly to people — as they were moving out on their own — breaking away from the tradition of huge state and collective farms, organized in the 1930's under Stalin.

Having been only a "cog in a larger machine" on the collective and state farms the early "private" farmers had little knowledge about running a farm and desperately needed examples, technical assistance and guidance.

Demonstration plots established on private farms were one of the ways to provide those things, especially in conjunction with short courses and loans.

Thus the demonstration plot program represented much more than showing farmers how to increase their potato yields. That was really only the part of it. Equally important, the plots motivated the farmers to seek more information through coursework at the Training and Education Center.

In order to secure operating loans, farmers were required to enroll in short courses and/or extension classes as a condition for securing such a loan.

RFCP's goal with the demonstration plots was not only to grow more and better potatoes but to grow the next generation of private farmers and rural leaders as well.

ESTABLISHING A TRUST FUND

It was becoming increasingly obvious with each passing day that, if the RFCP was to achieve anywhere near the goals it had set for itself, significant amounts of funds would need to be acquired and a financial entity established for receiving, managing and dispersing such funds.

With little real assurance regarding the source or magnitude of such funds, Hofstad and Danilenko preceded to set up such an entity in 1993 and named it the Russian Farms International Trust Fund. Its initial capital consisted of $3,000.00 (about 4,800,000 rubles at the time) — half of which came from Russians, and half from Americans.

The first Board of Trustees consisted of two Americans, Ralph Hofstad, and Lee Kolmer; and, two Russians, Andrei Danilenko and Victor Storozenko.

When RFCP's initiatives become sustainable, Russians will comprise a majority of the board.

The Trust Fund was registered in Russia and all of its funds must be utilized in Russia. The objective of the Trust Fund is to receive, manage, invest, and disperse funds used by the Russian Farm Community Project. All transactions are in accord with accepted business and financial principles and are neutral on political and religious matters.

Under the terms of the original agreement, the Trust Fund operates as a revolving fund in which all generated funds impact only the RFCP program.

The funds are primarily used to assist in the development and financing of agricultural projects. The goals of such funding are to:
- Assist the development of a sound economic infrastructure for the agricultural sector;
- Provide individual farmers and former state and collectivized farms and local businesses and entrepreneurs with financing, educational courses and the technical assistance needed to attain and sustain profitability.

The Trust Fund is not subject to U.S. or Russian taxes.

The main restriction on use of the funds is that the funds have to be invested in the Russian agricultural rural community sector. The exception is that any unused funds can be invested in government securities (GKO) and/or in the Russian securities equity market (Russian Trading System.) The funds invested in the RTC do not have to be connected to the agriculture sector.

RFCP has had two primary sources of investment - government

66

treasury bills (GKO) and RFCP's lending program. (More about the lending program later in this book.)

The general policy of the Trust Fund has been to invest funds into government treasury bills until they are needed.

The yields on the treasury bills have been as high as 150% in 1995 and as low as 25-30% in 1998. The general trend of yields has been downward, however.

The primary source of funds for the trust fund has been the U.S. government's Food for Progress Program although U.S. private sources have contributed over $350,000 per year as well.

The Food for Progress Program, and the amount sourced through this program, are described in the next section.

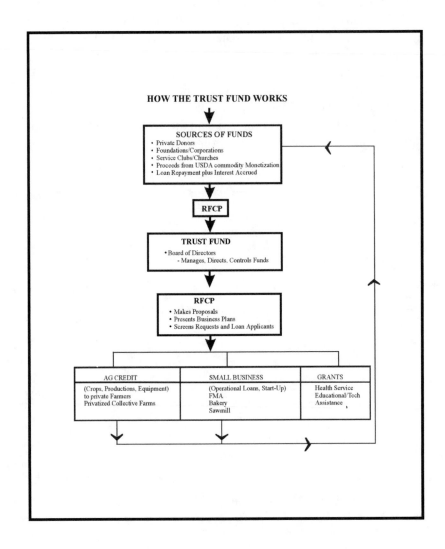

PARTNERING WITH THE U.S. GOVERNMENT

Someone once said, almost anyone can open a bank, the much more difficult part is finding the financial resources to give it life.

That was certainly the case with RFCP's trust fund, as it became obvious rather quickly that the "substantial funds" RFCP needed were not immediately available in the Dmitrov Raion, in greater Russia, or from private sources in the United States.

That left the U.S. Government, and its various international development and assistance programs, as the primary possibility for such funds and the timing seemed right for accessing them. It was early 1994, almost three years after the collapse of Communism and time enough for the U.S. government to have developed some "assistance programs," to assist the Russians in their transition to a free enterprise system.

Having been responsible for identifying and monitoring such U.S. government assistance programs while at Land O'Lakes, and indeed having secured and utilized a substantial amount of such funds for development purposes, it was my role to do a preliminary assessment of programs which might be compatible with RFCP's needs for funding.

That assessment indicated there were a number of such programs available in the Agency for International Development (AID); in the Overseas Private Investment Corporation (OPIC): the World Bank; and the United States Department of Agriculture (USDA). Only one program, "The Food for Progress Program" in the United States Department of Agriculture (USDA), really seemed to fit RFCP's immediate needs.

The "Food for Progress" program provides commodities for humanitarian and economic development programs in developing countries. Under the Food for Progress program, the USDA has authority to provide 500,000 metric tons of commodities and up to $30 million for non-commodity costs such as shipping the commodities to foreign countries each fiscal year.

To access these commodities, private non-profit international development organizations like RFCP needed to submit proposals to the Foreign Agriculture Service (FAS) of the USDA requesting a specified tonnage of commodities to sell (monetize) in another country. The proceeds of such sales are used for food assistance or economic development projects as described in the proposal that is submitted. USDA pays the costs of shipping the commodities to the specified country.

The FAS is responsible for receiving and reviewing the proposals and awarding commodities to those organizations which have submitted the "most worthy" proposals.

The good news was that this program seemed made to order for the Russian Farm Community Project, and could provide the "significant" amount of funds that it needed.

The bad news was that the Food for Progress program usually receives more requests for commodities than it could fund, and typically its funds are depleted before all of the worthy proposals are funded.

Proposals are usually reviewed in the order in which they are submitted. Being close to the top of the list is a distinct advantage. This was quite discouraging because by the time RFCP had decided to pursue this route for funding, upwards of 50 organization had already submitted proposals for that particular year.

On the surface, the situation seemed rather hopeless. But hopeless doesn't necessarily mean helpless. And so I began to wonder how the government might react if an organization like RFCP offered to pay some of the costs related to the commodities, for example, offering to pay the freight for shipping the commodities. Would this unheard of gesture move us closer to the head of the list?

A few calls to long-time friends in government provided me with the freight costs for shipping, say 10,000 metric tons of commodities, to Russia. The cost was $250,000.00.

Armed with that information, I went to Hofstad and said, "I think I know how we can move up on the USDA's list for Food for Progress commodities." His response was, "How in the world are we going to do that?" I replied, "Let's offer to pay the freight costs of $250,000.00." Quite a statement for someone with usually less than $20.00 in his billfold. But Hofstad was up to the challenge. Without batting an eye he said, "Let's do it. I have such a strong belief in this Project, I'll put up the money myself and worry about getting it back later."

So Hofstad and I went to Washington with our proposal and our $250,000 offer in hand and RFCP received a grant. "We have been blessed with a remarkable gift, and been presented with an equally remarkable challenge!" Hofstad commented, as he signed an extraordinary agreement with RFCP's latest partner, the United States Department of Agriculture in Washington, D.C.

Under the agreement, the U.S. government agreed to provide 10,000 metric tons of surplus commodities to RFCP to be sold in Russia. These commodities were expected to generate $1.5 million or more, which would go directly into the Project's International Trust Fund in Russia to support its agricultural development work. In return RFCP agreed to pay the U.S. government $250,000, representing the shipping costs to transport the commodities to Russia. On the positive side it meant that for every dollar raised by RFCP from private donors, the U.S. government was multiplying it SIX TIMES through this agreement. On the negative side, RFCP had to come up with $250,000 in 90 days.

And so in 1994, RFCP's partnership with the U.S. government began.

RFCP's proposal was accepted and the 10,000 MT of soybeans it received from USDA in 1995 netted RFCP $850,000 for the Project.

Subsequent proposals in 1996, 1997, and 1998 generated another $3,972,471 and RFCP didn't have to pay any more shipping costs.

From 1995 and through 1997, RFCP relied on Cooperative Business International (CBI), a Washington based organization serving U.S. cooperatives, to ship and sell the commodities it received under the Food for Progress program. After 1997 RFCP handled these functions itself.

71

PARTNERING WITH U.S.
DEVELOPMENT ORGANIZATIONS

The U.S. has long prided itself on its substantial economic development efforts throughout the world and well it should. Much of this work is performed by private U.S. development organizations (non-governmental organization or NGO's) which operate under grants from the U.S. government.

Four of the most notable U.S. development organizations, as it relates to food and agricultural development, are Cooperative Business International (CBI); Agricultural Cooperative Development International (ACDI); Volunteers for Overseas Cooperative Assistance (VOCA) and the Citizens Network for Foreign Affairs.

Among the government funds administered by these organizations are funds which are designated for the payment of expenses, and sometimes a small stipend, for volunteers working overseas for short periods of time (3-4 weeks) on approved development initiatives.

Since one of RFCP's goals was to recruit and send volunteer mentors to Russia for short periods as part of its development efforts, partnerships with these organizations was deemed critical to its success.

Thankfully, each of the organizations were willing to partner with RFCP and to date have provided funding for 47 volunteer mentor trips to Russia as part of RFCP's effort. Naturally, RFCP is most grateful for all they have done and particularly indebted to Robert "Bob" Clark, President and CEO of CBI, and his staff; Mike Deegan, President and CEO of ACDI/VOCA and his staff, and John Costello, President and CEO of the Citizens Network and his staff, for their willingness to partner with RFCP and for the advice, support and outstanding assistance their organizations have provided.

CBI deserves special mention, because, it also handled the monetization of commodities for RFCP in its early years. Moreover, when Clark became President and CEO of CBI and decided to terminate CBI's development initiatives to concentrate on commercial initiatives, he transferred CBI's development funds, in Russia, to RFCP (with USDA approval), and has provided the leadership for the development of a Farm Supplies and Services Center in support of RFCP's dairy initiatives.

PARTNERING WITH ROTARIANS

Rotary Clubs are located all over the world and in most of the larger U.S. cities and towns. They provide an opportunity for community leaders to work together in community service projects, and to assemble weekly for fellowship and to hear speakers talk about community, state and international happenings, issues and developments.

Through their local clubs, Rotarians get involved in a broad variety of service projects.

Through their international organization, Rotary International, they participate in humanitarian endeavors throughout the world – one of the most outstanding of which in recent years has been their initiative to eradicate polio from the face of the earth.

Hofstad, (Minneapolis Minnesota Rotary Club), Danilenko, (Moscow Rotary Club), Freeh (Roseville Minnesota Rotary Club), Moore, (Shoreview/Arden Hills Minnesota Rotary Club), and former board members Meigs, (St. Paul Minnesota Rotary Club) and Siemens, (Trail, British Columbia Rotary Club) are Rotarians. Their Rotary Clubs and the Wyzata Minnesota Rotary Club became partners with RFCP.

Through those partnerships the various clubs have provided computers and other equipment for RFCP's Training and Education Center; equipment for the new bakery in Dmitrov, funds for a sewing center, and a turkey project.

Thanks to the efforts of the Minneapolis and St. Paul Minnesota Rotary Clubs, the Moscow Rotary Club and their affiliated Rotaract Clubs, thousands of packages of bandages, surgical gloves, disposable clothing for newborns, blood transfusion systems and hundred of other medical supplies such as wheelchairs and hospital beds have been sent to children's hospitals in the Dmitrov Raion.

This joint RFCP/Rotary International service project is benefitting hundreds of children and adults in the Dmitrov Raion.

Currently the Roseville Rotary Club, and the Minneapolis #9 Rotary Club in Minnesota, and the Moscow and Dmitrov Rotary Clubs are sponsors of a 3-H Grant Proposal which has been submitted to the Rotary International Foundation requesting $350,000 over a three year period to help underwrite drug and alcohol abuse rehabilitation and prevention program for youth, and health care initiatives for infants, the elderly and the disabled in Dmitrov.

RFCP is most grateful for the assistance it has received from Rotary Clubs and Rotarians in America and in Russia.

LAUNCHING THE FIRST BUSINESS VENTURES

From the beginning, RFCP's over-riding goal has been to help the Russian people replace their centralized government owned and supported entities with privately owned profit generating businesses.

During its first two years in Russia, RFCP helped the Russians assess their resources and their needs. During that assessment the following profit generating businesses emerged as being immediately most beneficial to the local economy:

1. Sawmill and building supply center,
2. Bakery,
3. Farm supply and services center,
4. Food processing and marketing center, and
5. Farm equipment service and distribution center.

The sawmill and building center were given high priority because of the critical need for building supplies in the Raion. Moreover, a struggling sawmill already existed which could rather quickly be converted into a profit generating business creating new jobs and income. The administration of the Dmitrov Raion favored such a venture; a trained labor force was available, and a robust building boom was developing in the area.

After a feasibility study, the sawmill and building supply venture was launched in 1994 with three primary owners: the Bunyatino Joint Stock Company, which provided equity in the form of its present sawmill; i.e., building and equipment; the Administration (Governor) of the Dmitrov Raion who provided equity in the form of a forest (from which trees could be harvested) and RFCP which provided equity in the amount of $50,000 for renovating the current facilities and purchasing much needed new equipment.

In cooperation with the Timiryazev Agricultural Academy, RFCP also committed to providing a mentor and training courses.

It was understood that the equity provided by RFCP could be purchased by Bunyatino farm at anytime at the cost of the original investment plus an 8% annual return.

Each of the "partners" had representation on the board of directors.

Gary Buttermore, owner/operator of a small sawmill in Ogden, Iowa, was selected by RFCP as the project's mentor through a partnership with the Citizens Network for Foreign Affairs which covered his travel costs.

In 1995 RFCP helped launch another business, a bakery, by providing a loan to a Russian entrepreneur, Mr. Mikhail Osipov, to cover operating costs and the remodeling of a cafeteria which Osipov was converting into a bakery in Ramenýe.

In addition, Minnesota Rotary District 5960 provided Mr. Osipov with $32,700 to purchase new equipment.

Osipov provided the building and covered some of the building remodeling costs.

The bakery sells brown bread, french bread, and an assortment of rolls. It has been very successful.

It has a customer base of approximately 5,000 people within a 20 kilometer area with an additional 1,500 people coming into the area during the summer.

Besides selling fresh bread to people in the immediate area, the bakery also hopes to supply fresh bread to retail outlets in surrounding towns on a regular basis.

While these two businesses were being launched, RFCP's presence was being felt in other ways as well.

ESTABLISHING COMMUNITY INITIATIVES

Earlier in this publication, reference was made to two women from Akron, Ohio, (Susan Dudas and her mother, Beth Godard,) who played such a significant role in the early planning and implementation of the Russian Farm Community Project. What follows elaborates on what these two outstanding persons contributed. Quite simply, it is they more than anyone who provided the leadership for the "community" portion of the Russian Farm Community Project; thereby, freeing Hofstad and Danilenko and their staffs to concentrate their efforts on farm and agricultural initiatives.

Giving liberally of their time, talents, financial resources, and the passion they developed on their initial trip to Russia, Susan and Beth returned to Russia to ask the women in the three villages served by RFCP what they felt were the most critical needs in their communities. Four needs were identified by the Russian women: dental care, computer and English classes for their children, recreation equipment for youth, and new ways for them to generate income through home- based industries.

An assessment of the villages, directed by Susan and some Russian women, revealed that a number of the women had outstanding abilities in such things as sewing, embroidery, and knitting, but lacked materials, equipment and markets to turn their skills into profitable enterprises. The immediate task was to find ways and means for providing the things which were missing. And that is what Susan and Beth did. They began by helping the women to organize themselves into cottage industry-type operations, such as sewing; then they provided them with sewing machines, materials and thread, and finally they helped them find markets for their finished products in Russia and the USA. As a result of their efforts a number of home-based industries were launched.

In response to the request for better dental care, Susan took a group of dentists from the United States to Russia for ten days, at no cost to the Project, to determine how best to proceed with a dental initiative.

At the conclusion of their ten day trip, the assessment team offered two recommendations for improving the dental care in the rural areas being served by RFCP:

#1 Supply contemporary western style dental equipment and supplies to the areas, and

#2 Identify and sponsor a local Russian dentist and train him or her to provide the necessary dental services.

The team agreed that sending American or Western trained dentists to practice in Russia wasn't the answer. Rather it would be better to use Russian dentists to help the Russian build self-sufficiency and independence — two goals common to all RFCP initiatives.

And so Susan joined with Ludmila Burch from the Dmitrov region to establish a new dental clinic in Nasadkino staffed by a Russian woman dentist. In the process she and Ludmila demonstrated outstanding leadership, determination and cooperation, as they worked diligently to overcome numerous obstacles to achieve the wishes of the woman of the community for better dental care for their children.

The clinic, which was officially dedicated in the summer of 1996, is located on the second floor of an apartment building next to an existing medical clinic.

The village government donated labor and materials, installed new plumbing and electric wiring, replaced the floor, and sanitized the room.

RFCP helped underwrite the salary of the dentist and her assistant and purchased a dental chair, operating equipment, medical instruments, and supplies.

By 1998 the clinic had become sustainable and so, at an official ceremony that year, Danilenko deeded ownership and operation of the clinic to the local community.

With two of the "needs" of the Russian women's group having been met, Susan Dudas now turned to the final two needs the Russian women had identified: classes in computers and English and additional recreational equipment for their children and youth. While Susan worked to establish the dental clinic, her mother, Beth, focused on a need the Russian women hadn't mentioned - housing.

INVOLVING YOUTH
(TEENS UNITING GLOBALLY OR TUG)

Meeting the needs for classes in English and computers was easier than expected. Susan simply enlisted her friend, Ludmila, to teach the initial classes followed later by the recruitment of other "teachers" from the region.

Meeting the needs for recreational equipment required more thought and became a real testimony to Susan's creative vision.

She asked herself, "if it's for youth why not involve American youth in meeting this need? Why not work through the churches that are part of Christians Uniting in Global Mission, CUGM, the original founders of the Russian Farm Community Project, in recruiting young men and women who would be willing to go to Russia for a week to ten days and work with Russian youth in building, assembling, painting, and renovating recreational equipment?" What an experience for both the American and Russian youth. What an opportunity to build new relationships, and discard old misunderstandings. What an opportunity to involve the generation in Russia that is so critically important to Russia's successful transition from Communism to the Private Enterprise System.

The opportunities seemed awesome, but so did the difficulties. Would the Russian people go for such an idea? Would the CUGM churches? Would it be too costly? Would American youth and Russian youth wish to participate – and even pay some or all of their costs? Would she have enough time to do all that needed to be done given her many other activities?

Convinced that the pros of such a program far outweighed the cons – and having recruited her husband, David, to assist her, Susan moved ahead, overcame all of her doubts and difficulties and founded "Teens Uniting Globally" (TUG) which was to become one of the strongest and most fulfilling segments of RFCP.

In the summer of 1996, American teenagers, representing five states, went to Russia and *paid to work*. That's right! On August 8-16, nine American youth organized as TEENS UNITING GLOBALLY (TUG) joined Russian teenagers in constructing new playground equipment, and painting and repairing a village Russian Orthodox church. The church had been closed for over 70 years, and had reopened just two years before. "We had lots of fun, made new friends and found them to be warm and friendly people!" said Megan Smith of Eagan, Minnesota.

"The playground equipment we put together was a generous gift to the village children of Nasadkino by Virginia Spurling, a member of our church," said Mandy Shell from First Congregational Church, Akron, Ohio. "Once we got the playhouse and the slide set up the kids were all over it. We had a formal dedication planned, but they just couldn't wait."

Was language a barrier? "Not really, some of the Russians spoke a little English...and we communicated a lot with our hands, kinda like pantomime with a lots of laughs," said Vandy Scoates of Newport Coast, California. "We did have an interpreter for back-up."

The American teens paid for their transportation, lodging and meals and lived in the dorm facilities at a nearby community school.

Besides their work assignments, the American teens visited the homes of their new friends and got a taste of Russian rural life. They also toured the RFCP's sawmill, new family farms, the Training and Education Center, and assisted in the dedication of the new dental clinic and playground.

There was time to exchange ideas, and concerns as well. "After a while, I realized that our hosts didn't have many material things and they value what they have quite differently than we do. There is a different emphasis on what is treasured and what has worth, and it has more to do with relationships and living, than material possessions," one American teen observed.

The TUG program now in its fifth year, brings together young people from America and the Dmitrov Raion each year to "build bridges of understanding." Working together to accomplish a specific community project for youth, TUG participants develop a unique sense of relationship, trust and understanding.

More about the TUG program in Part V of this book.

BUILDING A FRIENDSHIP HOUSE

While Susan was founding TUG, Beth Godard was dreaming her own dream about housing. Given the shortage of housing in the Dmitrov region and the growing need for suitable quarters to house the increasingly greater numbers of mentors who were coming to the region as part of RFCP's efforts, she wondered, "why not build a guest house in the Dmitrov Raion for people coming from Moscow or the USA to help the people in Dmitrov?"

Unlike the movie "Field of Dreams" which promised that if an Iowa farmer built a baseball field on his farm, the players would come, Beth already knew the people were coming, and they needed housing. So she provided funds so it would be there for them. One beautiful late summer day in 1996, the Beth Godard Friendship House was dedicated and her dream became a reality just like her daughter, Susan's dreams.

"A place where friendships can grow . . . where farmers and mentors can gather." With head bowed, Rev. David Tyler Scoates, founding Director of the Russian Farm Community Project, prayed words of thanksgiving, which were simultaneously translated to area farmers, villagers, RFCP leaders from Minnesota and Moscow, the members of a tour group visiting the project, board members, and representatives of the Dmitrov Administrator's office and the U.S. Embassy in Moscow, who all linked hands in a huge prayer circle.

The ribbon-cutting ceremony was preformed by Mary Revelt of the U.S. Embassy in Moscow. Ms. Antonina, representing the Dmitrov Chief Administrator's office; and Beth Godard representing RFCP.

Near the front door, in a place of honor, a framed photo was hung showing Beth Godard being embraced by a Russian grandmother.

"We are two Babushkas!" laughed Godard, referring to herself and her new friend. "We met on the street when I was here in 1992...we just saw each other, smiled and hugged."

The photo has become a symbol of new relationships between the U.S. and Russia, and exemplifies the spirit of the RFCP.

A wooden plaque, identifying the friendship house, in both Russian and English, was placed at the front door.

Though he wasn't on the program, the response of one of the attending farmers pretty much summed up the feelings of all in attendance.

"We give thanks to the one who gave us this friendship house. Not only will the people who use it help us improve our agriculture, it will

help us to grow new friendships and deeper relationships."

The first official event in the house was the signing of a letter of agreement and understanding between Chief Administrator Gavrilov, Hofstad, and Danilenko to expand the working relationship between RFCP and the Dmitrov Raion.

The friendship house has a "homey" atmosphere with five sleeping rooms, a dining area, kitchen, and fireplace. The house is staffed by local villagers; thereby, bringing new revenue to the area's economy.

Two outstanding women, two outstanding mentors, from Ohio, Beth Godard and Susan Dudas dreamed some dreams and then made them come true and the Russian people are reaping the benefits.

1992 - 1994 IN REVIEW

- Established a number of important partnerships in Russia and the U.S.

- Developed the concept of a model infrastructure system to support agriculture, agri-business and the rural community.

- Established the Russian Farms International Trust Fund to handle all funds committed to the RFCP efforts in the Dmitrov District ($400,000 in private funds thus far.)

- Contracted with the Timiryazev Agricultural Academy in Moscow to provide technical assistance and training in the district.

- Converted an elementary school building in the village of Ramenýe into a training and educational center.

- Assisted in the development of a farm business plan for the Zarechenskoe Joint Stock Company.

- Offered short courses on bookkeeping, enterprise analysis, financing, credit, and business plans for farmers and entrepreneurs.

- Assisted in the planning and management of demonstration potato plots, some of which yielded increases of up to 300% over current potato production in the district.

- Assisted in the planning and management of a forage demonstration and feeding trial.

- The Governor of the Dmitrov District made 5,000 hectares of land available for the establishment of new family farms.

- Provided funding and mentoring for a sawmill and building supply center and a bakery.

- Partnered with VOCA, ACDI, CBI and Citizens Network to provide mentors and technical assistance for participants in the

RFCP project, in the Dmitrov Raion.

· Established community related initiatives and a youth program.

· Built a friendship house.

Dr. Robert Schuller and members of the exploratory group he and Dr. David Tyler Scoates took to Russia in 1992.

Scoates presiding at a meeting in one of the villages visited. Ralph Hofstad is on his immediate right and Robert Schuller and Andrei Danilenko on his left.

David Scoates and Ralph Hofstad in a moment of
relaxation.

Valery Shilin, Farm Manager of the Zarechenskoe
farm and Victor Storozhenko, Professor at the
Timiryazev Agricultural Academy, shake hands
with Ralph Hofstad, executive Director of RFCP
and pledge themselves to build a better agricultural
system in Russia.

Danilenko and Hofstad watch Governor Gavrilov put
his signature on the Memorandum of Agreement
between he Dmitrov Raion and RFCP. Valerie
Kuznetsov of the Russian RFCP team assists.

Dr. Otis Young, Chair of the RFCP board of directors, helps
Naomi Wilden and Antonina Dovrinova cut the ribbon for the
opening of the Education and Training Center.

Farmers at one of the first classes at the Education and Training Center. Victor Storozhenko is at the far left.

Professor J.T. Scott, right, of Iowa State University discusses the results at one of the first potato demonstration plots with some Russian staff members.

Russian farmer poses with some of the potatoes
from the
first demonstration plots.

Ralph Hofstad, Executive Director of RFCP, Gerald
Meigs, member of the RFCP board, Vern Freeh, member of the RFCP staff, and Walter Siemens, member of
RFCP board, all Rotarians, pose with the manager of
the new bakery. Equipment for the bakery was provided
through a grant from Minnesota Rotarians.

A closer look at some of the bakery's products.

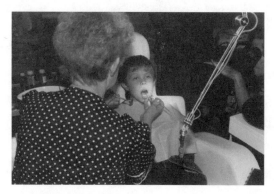

One of the first patients at the new dental clinic.

The new dentist enjoying her
surroundings.

Susan Dudas and Ludmilla
Burch at the dedication of the
dental clinic.

The author, Beth Godard, Susan Dudas, and Ralph Hofstad
at the dedication of the Friendship House.

The picture of Beth Godard and her Russian friend
which hangs in the friendship house.

Some of the Teens Uniting Globally group and
their new found friends.

PART V

GAINING MOMENTUM/THE MIDDLE YEARS

1995-1997

PROLOGUE

In the years 1995 to 1997, RFCP focused its efforts on further defining and refining the economic development model it was putting in place in the Dmitrov Raion.

It was also the period during which it separated from its parent organization, Churches Uniting in Global Mission (CUGM) and hosted a number of U.S. and Russian agricultural dignitaries and others who were becoming ever more interested in what RFCP was doing.

It was during this period that RFCP created a credit and lending program; developed and offered a broad range of courses and services at its training and education center, established a Farmers Marketing Association, utilized an ever growing number of U.S. mentors in its development efforts and did the necessary exploration, planning and groundwork for the establishment of a major dairy revitalization initiative, a farm supplies and services center, a business development center, and expanded community and youth initiatives.

SEPARATING FROM CUGM

In 1995 the Russian Farm Community Project filed for and received its own Certificate of Incorporation and essentially ended its direct relationship with Churches Uniting in Global Mission (CUGM).

The separation was thought to be in the best interests of both organizations since the Russian Farm Community Project was growing much faster and larger than the General Council of CUGM had envisioned.

Moreover while RFCP had been growing and expanding its initiatives in Russia, CUGM had substantially narrowed the focus of its mission to one of assisting churches and their ministers.

The terms of the separation were amicable and supportive:

- CUGM would continue to view the Russian Farm Community Project as one of the programs it had founded but would no longer be directly involved in its initiatives.
- CUGM would support RFCP's efforts in its newsletter and at its meetings and would encourage its member churches to stay involved with RFCP and its activities.
- RFCP would continue to list CUGM as its founder and keep CUGM and its members informed about its activities. RFCP's historic relationship with CUGM is important and highly valued.

U.S./RUSSIAN DIGNITARIES VISIT PROJECT

In the summer of 1995, U.S. Secretary of Agriculture Glickman visited the RFCP project, bringing the Russian Minister of Agriculture, Alexander Nazarchuk, with him.

Drs. Victor Storozenko, Yuri Izilov, Executive Director Ralph Hofstad, and Andrei Danilenko, guided the tour.

Amidst a swarm of cameras and reporters, Glickman and Nazarchuk toured three locations where RFCP has made a difference in the lives of farmers in the past 15 months; the first, a small sawmill, jointly owned by a privatized collective and the RFCP Trust Fund, which manufactures materials and supplies for the construction of log homes in the area. The sawmill also brought new jobs to the Bunyatino community. Next they walked the land at the farm site of the Vetrov family. In a one-on-one interview with farmer, Victor Vetrov, the ag leaders learned first-hand the difficult economic struggle faced by farmers who want to become independent farmers. Farm loans were no longer available from the government and bank loan interest had skyrocketed to 200%. Rather than receiving a high interest rate loan, Mr. Vetrov chose crop-sharing as an affordable loan alternative through RFCP. From the Russian coordinators of the Training and Education Center, Glickman and Nazarchuk learned of the 300% increases in potato production which were achieved on RFCP sponsored demonstration plots by combining American and Russian know-how. The following year these same methods were adopted by a local privatized collective farm and a private farmer to boost potato production.

Glickman and Nazarchuk were deeply impressed and pleased with RFCP's efforts and designated the Project as a model for the privatization of agriculture and rural communities in Russia.

Glickman described his visit to Dmitrov region as "one of the highlights of his trip to Russia." He also noted that information gleaned from the visit, provided important background for subsequent discussions with the Russian Minister of Agriculture.

> "I was able to gain an appreciation of the highly productive work you are doing and to pick up some insights into Russian agriculture as well...I am pleased that we are now supporting your work through our Food for Progress Program"
> — U.S. Agriculture Secretary, Dan Glickman

Since its beginning RFCP's efforts and accomplishments have been viewed by hundreds of Russian and American people interested in seeing what was being done.

In 1995, 96, and 97, RFCP offered self-funded tours for American people to visit the project site.

Almost 100 people took advantage of this opportunity to see what was being done.

CREATING A CREDIT AND LENDING PROGRAM

Determination and knowledge are important attributes for success and progress in any nation or culture. Equally important is capital.

In the Dmitrov Raion, RFCP found people who were determined to succeed, willing to acquire the knowledge they needed to succeed, and willing to work hard, but unfortunately there was very little capital available to support their determination. With 80 percent of the wealth located in Moscow, rural communities and agriculture were generally left to fend for themselves.

Not only was capital almost non-existent, the Russian government wasn't subsidizing or providing farm loans. Commercial banks charging up to 200% for three month business loans, were refusing to even consider farm loan requests because they were "too risky." As a consequence in the five years after the fall of Communism, 30,000 independent Russian farmers went bankrupt.

Such was the financial environment in which RFCP developed its credit and lending program.

The purpose of the lending program, in the words of Brian Foster (RFCP volunteer "mentor" and principle architect for the program) was "...to pump blood into the heart of Russia's agricultural future, the independent family farmer and private businessman and to encourage Russian banks to do the same."

"For some beginning farmers in Russia such a program would be the difference between putting in a crop or packing it in." And the 39 year-old Iowa farmer knew what he was talking about.

Foster, who with his wife Patricia, had raised hogs in Hampton, Iowa, after graduating from Iowa State University, knew all about the credit needs of U.S. farmers and learned about Russia's agricultural credit needs while serving as the Director of Volunteers of in Overseas Cooperative Assistance, (VOCA), in Russia for two years.

As a volunteer mentor for RFCP Foster interviewed a broad cross section of people about their credit needs. Based on those interviews and his personal insights, he recommended that agricultural and small business loans should receive the highest priority, and initial loans should be made to those having farming experience, access to land, machinery and facilities and a reasonable chance to succeed as private farmers.

He also recommended that RFCP should continue its investigation into marketing opportunities for Dmitrov Raion's private farmers and the possible creation of a marketing center.

Foster also recommended that RFCP and the Administration of the Dmitrov Raion establish a homesteading program similar to the one in the United States before the turn of the 20th Century.

Like the U.S. program such a program would provide homesteaders with parcels of land from the Dmitrov Raion Administration (government) which the homesteader would own after a period of years if the homesteader had successfully farmed and improved the land.

Plans for such a program were developed but to date have not been implemented.

PROVIDING LOANS AND CREDIT

Using Foster's research and recommendations as its guide, RFCP launched its credit and lending program in 1996. Six hundred thousand dollars were set aside for this initial effort. The funds came from the monetization of commodities received under the Food for Progress Program.

A revolving loan fund was established exclusively for private farmers needing money for the production of crops and/or the purchase of equipment, storage, etc.

The lending policies required that all loans had to be repaid with interest under the terms specified so the fund could grow and be available for an ever greater number of farmers in future years.

To participate in the program private farmers had to:
1. Submit a financial statement,
2. Prepare a business plan,
3. Participate in a family and farm management training program,
4. Maintain cost and revenue records and submit them to RFCP, and
5. Agree to assist beginning farmers, as mentors, if called upon to do so.

RFCP staff were available to assist potential borrowers with the preparation of their loan materials.

Applicants were encouraged to submit ideas relating to the procedure for receiving loan requests and establishing interest rates.

RFCP's plan called for the loans to be offered through a Russian bank, Agropromstroy, with RFCP paying a fee to the bank for handling the loans.

The RFCP staff developed the principles, policies, and interest rates under which the program operates and selected the loan recipients.

The initial loans were offered at a 4% per month interest rate and the loan program was publicized throughout the Dmitrov Raion.

MANY APPLY FOR LOANS

RFCP received scores of loan applications which the staff narrowed down to 18 applicants, who would receive the first loans.

One of those 18 was Inna Terekhina. Her request was for a loan to buy forage seed which she would plant in the spring, cut and bale as hay in the fall, and feed to her dairy cows in the winter. In the past the lack of good forage had seriously reduced the amount of milk produced by her cows. Her story is similar to that of other early private farmers in Russia.

"When economic reform came and private farming started in 1990, my husband and I jumped at the opportunity," says Inna, who was working as a nurse in Dmitrov at the time. Her husband, an electrician, had been raised in a rural village. They were city folk with a dream — to work for themselves and own their own farm business.

In November that year, she arrived early at the local government office and was the fourth to register as a private farmer, officially "a milk producer" for the region. She was granted land by the local government and became one of Russia's first private farmers — a somewhat bitter distinction, in that by 1994 over 30,000 of this new breed would have already thrown in the towel on private farming. Most failed because they lacked management skills, equipment, and credit, and government subsidies had been suspended.

"We started with one dairy cow, then seven, then eleven and now twenty-two," says Inna who tells proudly how her husband, "laid every brick to build each building on the farm, including their house." They now own 45 hectares and rent an additional 111 hectares.

The Terekhina's farm is a real family operation. Two school-age sons, plus grandma and grandpa, help to make the dream a reality. Besides milk, they also sell raspberries and cabbage from their garden, and are planting currants and developing an apple orchard. They are industrious, but need to produce more milk and generate more income.

Inna says 27 dairy cows is an optimum size for their farm. She doesn't want more cows. But she wants to increase the production per cow. She believes the forages they will grow as a result of this loan are critical to their success. She has learned to keep accurate diary records and knows her herd averages 7,700 lbs of milk per year (compared to U.S. herd yields which are twice to nearly three times this amount.) Two of her cows produce over 13,200 lbs of milk each per year, so there is hope.

101

But the family's entrepreneurship doesn't stop with production. Inna is becoming aware of what we know as "niche marketing." To get better prices for their milk, Inna sells it locally. About half is picked up by customers for cash at the homestead as farm-fresh milk. The rest is delivered to homes in nearby Dmitrov. She says people are willing to pay more for fresh milk. The demand is there if she can just keep increasing the supply. Positive about the potential for others in her business, she smiles, "I'm optimistic for the future," she says and predicts, "The Moscow market is very good, very large and receptive to creative marketing."

Farming hasn't been all roses for the Terekhinas. In 1993, they bought 13 "pedigree" cows — or so they thought. Unfortunately, only one was actually pedigreed and a good producer. From that cow they are building their herd for the future. The RFCP loan was a significant stepping stone toward that goal of increasing herd milk production.

Proud of the new family farm, Inna is hopeful her children will one day be private farmers in the new Russia she is helping to establish.

The initial lending program in 1996 was designated for short term crop production loans only. In 1997 the program was expanded to include livestock operating loans and small business lending. $1 million was made available for lending.

Eighty percent of the borrowers paid back their loans in 1996. In 1997 only 70% were able to pay back on schedule, because of lower crop yields and drier weather conditions. These loans were refinanced and carried over to the next year.

From the onset of its credit and lending program RFCP knew it couldn't possibly meet all of the capital needs for farmers in the Dmitrov Raion. Rather the goal was to demonstrate that given half a chance and favorable interest rates, farmers could prosper and help grow the economy of their area with minimal risk to lenders.

The hope was that, seeing the favorable experiences of the RFCP lending program, the local government and banks would begin to respond to the credit needs of farmers, and through competition, would significantly reduce the interest rates.

While there has been some progress, this hope remains largely unfulfilled.

FARMERS' MARKETING ASSOCIATION

When it happened, the establishment of the first Russian Farmers' Marketing Association (FMA) in Russia happened quickly. The date was March 4, 1997. The place, the RFCP Training and Education Center in Ramenýe. There were about 20 farmers present.

Vern Moore, RFCP staff member, had just completed a seminar on farmers' marketing associations and Andrei Danilenko had just begun a group discussion on how the farmers in the Dmitrov Raion would organize such an association, when one of the farmers suggested they should do it now. The need was great so why wait.

Within the next half hour the group had elected a Board of Directors and had taken several other actions which would serve to legalize their decisions and set the whole process into motion.

The new board met three days later on Friday, March 7, 1997 and elected Inna Terekhina as its first chair. Perhaps another first; the first woman elected to chair such a board in Russia.

Since this all sounds rather spontaneous with little aforethought, the formation of the association was actually proceeded by a year of research and planning.

In the spring of 1996, Cheryl Hensley, a U.S. marketing specialist, was provided to RFCP by one of its partner organizations, (the Citizens Network for Foreign Affairs), to research the possibility and feasibility of establishing a farmer-owned marketing association in the Dmitrov Raion.

In assessing the need, Hensley interviewed a cross section of the 288 private farmers in the Raion, and found they were seriously disadvantaged when it came to marketing their products. Only 50 or 60 farmers were considered strong enough to survive on their own.

Under the old Communist system there were no private farmers, and all agricultural production was marketed through the state controlled distribution centers.

Now private farmers had to compete against the much larger joint stock companies (converted state and collective farms) and state controlled enterprises.

Those enterprises, even though grossly inefficient, still had the old market system at their disposal which gave them a distinct marketing advantage over private farmers.

It was Hensley's conclusion that the private farmers would fail if they didn't unite in their marketing efforts.

Hensley recommended that RFCP help interested private farmers in the Dmitrov Raion organize themselves into a farmers' marketing association and provide some initial financing for the association.

It was on this basis that the Dmitrov FMA was born on March 4, 1999.

The association decided to concentrate its initial efforts on the marketing of potatoes. They also decided that in their marketing efforts they would take possession, (but not title) to the potatoes and act as a brokerage agent for its members.

But first they needed to hire a manager and staff, conduct a comprehensive analysis of potential markets in the area, develop a marketing plan, and establish some marketing contracts.

For its farmer members, they needed to organize marketing short courses and seminars, explore possible other crops which might do well in the Dmitrov Raion, and assist farmers in acquiring the supplies they would need for raising their products.

They looked to RFCP for assistance in each of these areas.

The association began with 13 private farmers and three joint stock companies as its founding members.

Voting rights were restricted to one vote per member.

However, distribution of retained earnings would depend on patronage usage.

The board was careful to allow only those who really believed in the association concept to become members.

The initial membership fee (one time fee) was $500.00 with the total membership investment in the association being $8,000 (13 private farmers and three joint stock companies.)

RFCP helped the association members to understand the value of a marketing association and how best to get one organized.

Under Communism there were similar types of organizations, but they were entirely state owned and operated.

RFCP stressed that for the association to be a success the membership needed to work together toward a common goal: they needed strong and fair leadership, a strong and competent manager and staff, a quality product offered to the consumer at a reasonable price, access to fair and reasonable credit, a variety of marketable products over time and a strong legal foundation.

RFCP provided the association with some start-up financing in the form of a $60,000 loan.

The bottom line was that RFCP would do all it could to help the

104

association succeed. In fact, it was up to the members to assure its success. That required that they work hard and as a team to make it happen.

Bad News and Good News

Unfortunately, even after all the study, educating, financing and good intentions, the Farmers Marketing Association failed. That's the bad news! Why did it fail? Most probably because the board of directors didn't spend enough time preparing themselves and the members prior to launching the association, didn't work hard enough to make it work, and became an operating board rather than a policy board.

The good news is that a second Farmers Marketing Association was launched in 1999 under new leadership, in conjunction with opening of the processing and distribution center described in Part VI of this book. This association is doing well.

PARTNERING WITH DMITROV GOVERNMENT REAFFIRMED AND EXPANDED

In May of 1997 the Administration of the Dmitrov Raion reaffirmed and expanded its partnership with RFCP with the following letter of cooperation and understanding. The partnership was further solidified and expanded with an additional agreement by the same parties in December of 1997.

See appendix V and VI

SEEING IS BELIEVING

Since its beginning RFCP's efforts and accomplishments have been viewed by hundreds of Russians and Americans who were interested in seeing what was being done.

In 1995, 96, and 97, RFCP offered tours for Americans wanting to visit the project site.

The tour participants came from throughout the United States and Canada — people from all walks of life ranging in age from 92 to 40. They came with one common interest, to visit Russia and most especially the Russian Farm Community Project.

They came and they saw Russians reopening and rebuilding their churches. They saw art galleries and museums being revitalized and refurbished. They saw entrepreneurs starting new businesses and new farms. They saw state and collective farms being restructured and redirected as stock companies. They saw first hand what was being accomplished by the Russian Farm Community Project. They met with some of the recipients of the loans that have been awarded through the Project's Trust Fund. They saw the bakery, the sawmill, and the Training and Education Center all started with funds from the Trust Fund. They participated in the dedication of the new dental clinic. They saw the friendship house built by the Project to accommodate people from American and Russia who go to the Project site to assist the people in this region.

They met with American teenage groups (TUG), (sponsored by the Project), who were constructing a playground, refurbishing a Russian Orthodox Church (which for years served as a granary), and the building a fence around a hockey rink.

They met with the women who had established a Sewing Enterprise — a cottage industry initiated by a gift of sewing machines and marketing ideas provided by the project.

They met with Russian Orthodox priests, with entrepreneurs, and with villagers. They heard the Russian people tell how much the Project's "Partnering for Peace and Progress" efforts meant to them and what was being accomplished.

They made new friends in Russia and they became close friends with each other. They came and they saw the benefits of U.S. and Russian people working together.

They left their homes as strangers and they returned as friends committed to the work of the Russian Farm Community Project.

107

Perhaps their reactions can best be summed up by the comments of a member of one of the tours, John Bowser of Meadville, Pennsylvania, who was there with his wife, Toni, "When I first heard of this tour, I felt it might be somewhat overpriced and overvalued. That feeling has changed 180 degrees. If anything it was underpriced and undervalued. The experiences we have had, the people we have met, the things we have seen, the memories we will always have, will be an important part of our lives forever."

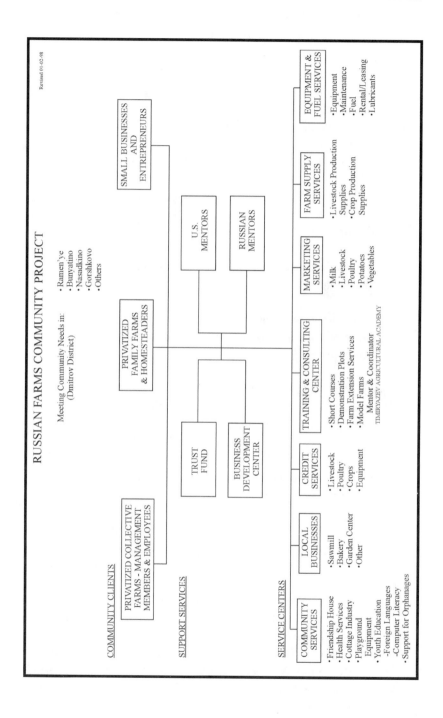

RUSSIAN FARMS COMMUNITY PROJECT

Revised 01-02-98

Meeting Community Needs in:
(Dmitrov District)
· Ramen'ye
· Bunyatino
· Nasadkino
· Gorshkovo
· Others

COMMUNITY CLIENTS

PRIVATIZED COLLECTIVE FARMS - MANAGEMENT MEMBERS & EMPLOYEES

PRIVATIZED FAMILY FARMS & HOMESTEADERS

SMALL BUSINESSES AND ENTREPRENEURS

U.S. MENTORS

RUSSIAN MENTORS

SUPPORT SERVICES

TRUST FUND

BUSINESS DEVELOPMENT CENTER

SERVICE CENTERS

COMMUNITY SERVICES
· Friendship House
· Health Services
· Cottage Industry
· Playground Equipment
· Youth Education
  -Foreign Languages
  -Computer Literacy
· Support for Orphanages

LOCAL BUSINESSES
· Sawmill
· Bakery
· Garden Center
· Other

CREDIT SERVICES
· Livestock
· Poultry
· Crops
· Equipment

TRAINING & CONSULTING CENTER
· Short Courses
· Demonstration Plots
· Farm Extension Services
· Model Farms
  Mentor & Coordinator
TIMIRYAZEV AGRICULTURAL ACADEMY

MARKETING SERVICES
· Milk
· Livestock
· Poultry
· Potatoes
· Vegetables

FARM SUPPLY SERVICES
· Livestock Production Supplies
· Crop Production Supplies

EQUIPMENT & FUEL SERVICES
· Equipment
· Maintenance
· Fuel
· Rental/Leasing
· Lubricants

109

SUMMARY OF ACCOMPLISHMENTS
1995 - 1997

The years 1995-1997 were busy and fulfilling years for the Russian Farms Community Project.

·   Processed 22 loans ($1,000,000)
-    18 private farm loans
-    1 bakery loan
-    3 joint stock company farm loans

·   Contracted with a bank to process the paperwork for loans and distribute and receive repayment of the funds.

·   Succeeded in getting the Governor to guarantee the loans (Russian-style.)

·   Employed a full-time extension agent officed at theTraining and Education Center to make regular calls on all farms and follow-up on loans.

·   Conducted 12 agriculture training courses at the Training and Education Center. Demonstration plots for potatoes, corn, wheat, and cabbage were completed and the results recorded and put into newsletter form for mailing and future teaching material. Field days were held to show the results to the farmers. A post-harvest seminar was held for farmers, education, government officials, and the media.

·   Farm leaders worked with RFCP staff and the Russian Ministry of Agriculture to create the most favorable cooperative structure for a Farmers' Marketing Association.

·   Signed a Letter of Cooperation and Understanding with the Dmitrovsky Joint Stock Company Farm which has acquired some rights to a marketing and distribution center from the city of Moscow. The plans are to partner with Dmitrovsky and locate the newly created Farmers Marketing and Supply Association on this site.

110

· Completed the initial investigation for the creation of a model restructured privatized collective farm, and taking a bankrupt agricultural joint stock company to sustainable profitability.

· A plan was developed for a Business Development Center which would include business, financial and consulting services, and a provision that a percentage of its future earnings be dedicated to building capital for the center.

· The Community Development Program, under the leadership of Susan Dudas and her assistant, Ludmila Burch, had a busy and productive year as they:

   a.   Opened a dental office in Nasadkino.
   b.   Organized a "TUG" tour (Teens Uniting Globally) for American teenagers to build bridges of understanding with the Russian youth.
   c.   TUG installed new playground equipment.
   d.   TUG assisted in cleaning and white washing a newly opened Russian Orthodox Church built by farmers in 1844.
   e.   Initiated English language and computer literacy courses.
   f.   Brought donated sewing machines to the Raion, and started a cottage industry to provide a new source of income for villagers.

· Sponsored two successful adult project tours people lead by Vern and Lois Freeh in 1996 and by Vern and Shirley Moore in 1997.

· Preliminary plans and assessments were made for a major dairy initiative.

Governor Gavrilov welcoming U.S. Secretary of
Agriculture Dan Glickman and Russian Minister of
Agriculture Alexander Nazarchuk to the training and
education center.

Secretary Glickman and Minister Nazarchuk are
welcomed by a villager in folk dress who presented
bread and salt – traditional symbols of
Russian hospitality.

Glickman visits the sawmill with Danilenko, left and Hofstad, right.

The top leaders for U.S. and Russian agriculture take a few minutes to discuss what they have seen.

Inna Terehina, one of the first recipient's of a RFCP
loan with some of her cows.

The Terehina farm buildings which were built
"brick by brick" by Inna's husband.

Another loan recipient, Vasily Soloviev, with Ralph
Hofstad. He used his loan to begin a fish farm.

Victor Vetrov, loan recipient, with his twin sons in
front of their barn.

John Vrieze, Baldwin, Wisconsin dairy farmer, RFCP
board member and team leader for the RFCP dairy
initiatives, discussing his dairy operations with
Hofstad; Project Coordinator, Andre Kravchenko, and
Andrei Danilenko.

Danilenko and Hofstad hold a kitchen meeting with
Nikolai and Julia Moskvin on the new dairy farm.

Andre Kravchenko, Chief Financial Officer and overall coordinator for the dairy initiatives with Nikolai Moskvin, owner of Razdolye dairy farm where RFCP's dairy initiative was launched.

The new free stall dairy barn on the Razdolye farm.

The cows enjoying their new surroundings.

Hofstad and Danilenko present Governor Gavrilov with a
ceramic cow and a symbolic check for $60MM to launch
the diary initiative in the Dmitrov Raion.

The Honorable James Collins
(second from the right),
U.S. Ambassador to Russia, visits the dairy project.

Mike Deegan, President and CEO of ACDI/
VOCA visits the Vrieze farm in Wisconsin
with Danilenko, Hofstad and Kravchenko.

Brian Foster, Chief Architect of RFCP Credit and
Lending program, on his Iowa farm with one of
his new born pigs.

PART VI

APPROACHING SUSTAINABILITY/
THE RECENT YEARS

1998-2000

PROLOGUE

The period 1998 to the present saw RFCP move ever closer to the sustainability goals it had set for itself. But it also saw those initiatives severely impacted by developments in Russia and America which had the potential of derailing RFCP's initiatives just short of sustainability.

On the horizon in 1998 were the final pieces that would comprise the RFCP economic development model:

·   a major dairy initiative,
·   a marketing and distribution center and farmers marketing association,
·   a new farm supply and marketing center,
·   additional partnerships,
·   a new business development center,
·   management of a bankrupt former collective farm,
·   expanded youth and community health initiatives, and
·   an opportunity to develop similar economic development models in other areas in Russia.

The future looked very bright.

Unfortunately three unforeseen developments lay just ahead — all with the potential for significantly impacting RFCP's plans and initiatives in a very negative manner.

The first of these developments was Russia's major financial crisis in 1998; the second related to delays in the shipment of RFCP's monetizable grain also in 1998; and the third was the U.S. government's decision to no longer provide monetizable commodities for economic development programs; choosing instead, to offer such monetizable commodities for humanitarian purposes only in 1999 and 2000.

As this is written, RFCP staff are in serious conversations with U.S. government officials to see if this decision can't be changed.

RUSSIA'S FINANCIAL SITUATION IMPACTS RFCP

Russia's year to start experiencing real economic growth and prosperity was supposed to be 1998. The economy was poised for 2-3% GDP growth after seeing a modest 0.4% growth in 1997, and inflation was less than 1% per month. But as those optimistic predictions were made, several lingering problems also became apparent, i.e., the Asian financial crisis leading to capital flight in the "emerging markets" - a large budget deficit leading to heavy short-term borrowing; a repressive tax system leading to less than expected tax revenues; high wage arrears leading to frustrated and angry workers; low oil prices leading to lower than expected export earnings; and most importantly and the continued financial mismanagement/corruption in both private business and government leading to a wider gap between the rich and poor.

These problems not only put the brakes on any growth potential, but slid the entire political and economic spectrum into chaos. This slide really accelerated with the firing of Prime Minister Victor Chernomyrdin in March of 1998. His replacement, Sergei Kirienko, was unable to stop the panic that had already started to engulf the country. This led to the August 17th disaster when the Russian government floated the ruble, and at the same time put a debt moratorium on its short-term debt load. This set off financial meltdown:

- The **ruble** dropped from 6.29 per dollar on August 17th to 15.-8000 on October 7th - a 151.2% decrease.
- The **equity market (RTS)** dropped from 109.43 on August 17th to 41.05 on October 7th - a decrease of 167%. The equity market was 411.61 at the beginning of the year - a drop of 90% and then the banks crashed.

123

AUGUST 17, 1998 – THE DAY THE RUSSIAN BANKS CRASHED

When the Russian banks crashed on August 17, 1998, RFCP was caught in a real dilemma. It was awaiting the transfer of almost $5 million from NCBA/CBI, representing some of the proceeds from commodities NCBA/CBI had monetized for RFCP in 1996 and 1997, as well as additional funds NCBA/CBI was transferring to RFCP because NCBA/CBI had decided to discontinue its development efforts in Russia.

Three and a half million dollars (which were to be transferred) were in an Inkombank account in Voronesh. The question was — Could those funds be retrieved and, if so, how much and by what means?

Even before the August 17th crash, Russian banks were notorious for mismanagement, and Inkombank was unfortunately one of the more notorious. The Russian government did little to prevent the crash and actually may have caused it to happen. First, by not following through with needed banking and other types of reform measures, and second, by placing a debt moratorium on its own securities. By doing so, the government, (in essence), made most of the larger banks insolvent, since a huge share of their portfolio was in the form of government security (GKO's - OZFs). In order to fund its budget deficits the government encouraged and sometimes required, the larger banks to purchase government securities.

Since the government didn't have any anti-crisis plan for taking care of the banking mess there was no was no clear way for individuals, or businesses to get their money out of banks like Inkombank. It became a matter of who you knew, and how much pressure an individual/business could exert on its bank, or possibly on the Central Bank. At the time of the crash, Inkombank owed the federal budget a substantial amount of money, so, all funds on deposit were frozen.

Actions for Retrieving Funds

The situation looked GRIM, to say the least, but not hopeless. A number of foreign organizations tried to get funds out, but none were able to do so. No one knew how long the process would take — nobody was even attempting to take a guess. Some thought it would take a minimum of six months to straighten out the mess, and that was being conservative. Even the signature of the President of Inkombank didn't

124

help one organization get its funds out. Nobody was sure who had control; whether it was under Central Bank control, or still under the control of Inkombank management.

Any transfer between banks has to pass through the Central Bank. On August 18th an attempt was made to wire transfer 1,687,450 rubles ($262,433) from the Voronish Inkombank account to the Trust Fund's Moscow account at Crystal Bank. The transfer did not occur. A written message from the Central Bank stated that the transfer, in essence, was frozen in Inkombank's debt account. The debt account was currently negative, and the funds would be released only when the balance became positive.

RFCP's next plan, drafted by Andrei Danilenko and his staff was for the Trust Fund to open an account at the Voronesh Inkombank branch, transfer the funds to this new account, and then try to use Trust Fund pressure to transfer the funds to the Crystal Bank account. Two of RFCP's Trust Fund staff went to Voronesh to try to clear up the problem, but without success. Inkombank said that they could not transfer any funds since all accounts were frozen.

Danilenko and his Russian staff then went to PLAN 2 which was to open an account at Inkombank's branch office in Moscow, and then try to transfer funds to a new Sherbank account. They had heard that there was a special arrangement between Sherbank and Inkombank for doing so because of the government's intent to get as many funds as possible to Sherbank, which was controlled by the government, and was the largest most stable bank in Russia at that time. There seemed to be no other option. Other U.S. organizations were trying to do the same thing.

On October 8, 1998, Danilenko received word that two million dollars was being sent to RFCP's Moscow account. The transfer would take a few days, at best, and possibly a week. The two million U.S. dollars was for the 1997 program. Once the funds were in our Sherbank account it was Danilenko's intent to get as many of those funds as possible out of Russia and into a U.S. bank for safekeeping.

Potential Losses

Once the funds were transferred to the Inkombank branch office in Moscow, the next step was to try to transfer the funds to Sherbank. Since bank-to-bank transfers had to be processed through the Central Bank, the Central Bank could hold up the transfers. If the funds were transferred, there would probably be some loss/discount. It was

Danilenko's intent to negotiate the best possible deal. The good news was that once the funds were in RFCP's account at Sherbank it would be possible to maintain their dollar value.

Under the circumstances, a discount between 6-10% would be considered a miracle, and between 11-20% unlikely. Transferring the funds to the U.S. from Inkombank was impossible, but there were several options from Sherbank. Many companies were pulling funds out of Inkombank at a 50% loss and considering it a good deal. The situation was extremely unpredictable, but RFCP was prepared to take all necessary actions to retrieve and protect its funds.

Recourse

While all this was happening, Danilenko and his Russian staff, working with anyone who might be helpful, also explored retrieval of the funds through the court system. This method was quickly rejected because a court case, especially of this magnitude could take months and maybe years before it was resolved.

The 10 days after the bank crash were most difficult for the RFCP's U.S. and Russian staff members who worked almost around the clock to protect and access its funds which were frozen in the Inkombank and had come under the receivership of the Central Bank (CB).

The situation was exacerbated by the fact that RFCP was being told that there was almost a 100% chance that Inkombank would declare bankruptcy, in which case all or certainly most of RFCP's money would be unrecoverable and that which was recoverable wouldn't be available for months or even years.

Faced with that information the Russian and U.S. staff spent most of their time looking for other ways to retrieve RFCP's funds before Inkombank went under.

The following is a summary of what was done:

Monday, October 12, 1998

RFCP was told that the "going rate" for retrieving funds from some insolvent banks in Russia was as high as an 80% discount. This was deemed unacceptable.

Tuesday, October 13, 1998

RFCP's Russian staff located a company called Itera (which is affiliated with the Russian company Gasprom) which said it could retrieve RFCP's funds and pay RFCP off in U.S. dollars, under the following conditions:

#1 Retrieval in equal payments over a one year period at a 15% discount.

#2 Retrieval in equal payments over a six month period at a 30% discount.

Itera was asked to provide RFCP with a promissory note to that affect.

The deal looked good on the surface but just in case the RFCP staff did a "due diligence" on the company, and had an independent organization do a "due diligence" on them as well, and learned the following:

Itera is an American based company owned by Russians. RFCP was not able to find any adequate financial information on the company, nor a banking guarantee that it could be satisfied with. During the process of RFCP's investigation, Itera withdrew the 15% over one year offer.

Wednesday, October 14, 1998

Given the reluctance of Itera to provide RFCP with financial information, discussions with them were discontinued.

In the meantime, RFCP's Russian staff learned that Agropromstroy bank, which had been handling RFCP's loan program for the last four years, indicated that it could retrieve the funds from Inkombank at a 50% discount, in U.S. dollars, immediately.

During this entire process Hofstad and Danilenko were in daily contact with Bob Clark, President and CEO of CBI, and our Russian staff had been in contact with CBI's Russian staff to assure that RFCP's fund retrieval efforts were coordinated with CBI's efforts, even to the point of joint handling of fund retrieval efforts to secure a more favorable discount.

Thursday, October 15, 1998

This day was spent examining and finalizing a contract with Agropromstroy bank and coordinating those efforts with CBI, which was considering a proposal developed through Rabobank at similar discount conditions.

Friday, October 16 to Monday, October 19, 1998

RFCP's staff were in the final stages of developing a contract with Agropromstroybank which called for the retrieval of at least $2.5 million of the CBI funds from the Inkombank in Voronesh. This would net RFCP $1,250,000.00.

All this was done under threat of losing all the funds CBI had in Inkombank if Inkombank declared bankruptcy. In the process, RFCP lost at least $2 million in U.S. dollars. Most other development organizations lost all their funds.

The $1,250,000.00, along with the projected proceeds from the sale of 1998 monetized grain plus funds from the repayment of outstanding loans, made it possible for RFCP to proceed with its planned projects and stay solvent for the next six months at least.

The main concern was the maintenance and appropriate use of the funds generated from the sale of the commodities under the Food for Progress Program and the continuance of RFCP's efforts in Russia.

In Russia the feeling was that what happened was bound to happen sooner than later, and maybe now the Russian government would get serious about building a real economy instead of the "artificial one" created by the banking and financial institutions. In order for the country's economy to fully develop, a solid production base needed to be built and the Russian Farm Community Project was hitting the "target" by putting its emphasis on production.

With the funds they were able to retrieve from Inkombank safely deposited in a U.S. bank, Hofstad and Danilenko hoped they could breath a bit easier, at least for a while. Not so!

Unfortunately, more problems lay just ahead only this time generated by U.S. policies.

THE SHIP BREAKS DOWN THREE TIMES

Even before almost losing its funds because of Russia's financial crisis, other difficulties were beginning to appear which would have a significant impact on RFCP's availability of funds. Only these were generated by U.S. policies involving the shipment of government owned commodities to Russia for monetization.

Here's what happened and its impact on RFCP.

In August of 1997, RFCP submitted a proposal to the U.S. government requesting 30,000 metric ton of hard Red Winter Wheat for monetizing in Russia. The Russian market price for wheat at that time was $180.00 U.S. dollars per metric ton. Therefore $3.5 million could be realized by RFCP from the monetization.

The proposal was approved in November of 1997, but for a number of reasons never specified by the U.S. government, the agreement for the wheat shipment was not ready for signing until June of 1998. By that time the market price in Russia had dropped to $145.00 U.S. dollars per metric ton. A decrease of $35.00 per metric ton in the amount that could be generated by RFCP through the sale of the wheat.

But it got even worse. Some years ago America's strong labor lobby was able to get a bill passed which decreed that 75% of all government owned commodities which are shipped by an ocean going vessel needed to be shipped on American ships (called U.S. bottoms) to protect the U.S. shipping industry.

The problem is that U.S. ships are often not as reliable as foreign ships (foreign flags.) This was certainly true of the ship chosen to ship RFCP's commodities to Russia which broke down three times en route to the Port of St. Petersburg. The end result was that despite all of the good work by our freight forwarder, James Meade of Daniel F. Young, the breakdowns delayed the arrival of the ship another month and by the time it arrived it was infected with insects because of the delay and handling problems.

The end result was that when the shipload of commodities (wheat) finally arrived in Russia, right in the middle of the financial crisis, the market price for wheat in Russia had fallen to $45.00 U.S. dollars per metric ton. This represented a loss of $100.00 per metric ton or a total of $2.5 million from the time RFCP submitted its proposal and the wheat was sold in Russia. Judicious planning, belt tightening, private donations, and loan repayment funds would need to carry the load until more funds could be generated from future monetized funds.

129

RFCP REAFFIRMS ITS COMMITMENT

While all this was happening, Hofstad was often asked if he didn't feel it was about time to pull out of Russia. His reply was classic Hofstad:

"Having seen a number of John Wayne movies in my life, I recall that in each of his movies someone at some point, when things got difficult, would ask him if he had had enough. In each case his answer would be an emphatic 'Not hardly!'

I feel that same way when asked if RFCP is giving any consideration to pulling out of Russia, given recent developments.

In 1993, when we made a commitment to help the people of the Dmitrov Raion privatize their agriculture and their rural communities, we entered into a commitment much akin to wedding vows — for better or worse — through good times and bad times, and we plan to honor that commitment. Friends do not leave their friends behind in times of trouble, because that's when the need is often the greatest.

While it's true that Russia is experiencing some difficult economic and political times, we are convinced that things will improve, and the efforts we have initiated with our Russian counterparts will grow, take root, and flourish.

I see that promise in people like Valery Gavrilov, Head of Administration of the Raion in which we have been working, who has given us tremendous encouragement, support, and assistance; I see it in Russian farmers and businessmen who have been recipients of RFCP loans; I see it in the farmer owned marketing organization we helped organize; in the model farm supply center, and the processing, marketing and distribution center; I see that promise in the TUG program, (Teens Uniting Globally), organized by Susan Dudas of Akron, Ohio and is now being lead by Pastor Norm Broadbent of the Falcon Heights United Church of Christ, Falcon Heights, Minnesota; I see it in the dental initiatives organized by Susan Dudas and the health initiatives being introduced under the leadership of Dr. Norman Westhoff and Doug Aretz of Minnesota; I see it in the rather extensive dairy initiative we are launching to demonstrate how the negative trends in the dairy industry can be reversed; I see that promise in the Russian people, our staff, the many U.S. volunteers and the U.S. government officials who help us, and the U.S. development organization with whom we are partnering.

RFCP move out of Russia? Not hardly!"

PARTNERING WITH A U.S. UNIVERSITY

As plans for RFCP's major dairy initiative were taking shape in early 1998, it became increasingly clear that management training in dairying would be critically important to the initiatives' success. Some of that training capability was available at RFCP's Russian University partner the Timiryazev Agricultural Academy, but more was needed.

So Hofstad and Danilenko and their staffs asked themselves the question, "Why not bring a distinguished American university into the partnership and capitalize on the capabilities of both?"

Such a university was found near the U.S. headquarters of RFCP in Minnesota, the University of Minnesota and its College of Agricultural, Food and Environmental Sciences.

And so in the fall of 1998 the University of Minnesota's College of Agricultural, Food and Environmental Sciences, the Timiryazev Agricultural Academy and the Russian Farm Community Project signed a Memorandum of Agreement and became partners for the purpose of expanding educational offerings for Russian farmers in the area of dairy management.

The Dairy Management Training Program concentrates on the most important missing link in the industry – *dairy management,* by introducing *a training and management know-how component as well as specific management tools – dairy management software,* which will be instrumental in training and educational efforts.

The goal of the program in Russia is to disseminate the knowledge of modern dairy management practices, which lead to sustainable and profitable dairy operations.

The program has the following objectives (as described in Section 19 of the Agreement):

> · *Develop a training program for trainers – dairy management faculty staff of Timiryazev Agricultural Academy in Moscow, Russia, in conjunction with the University of Minnesota and dairy business experts.* Selected 3-4 Russian candidates will acquire theoretical, practical and methodological knowledge and skills through the 2-month long intensive dairy management training program in the United States.

> · *Expected outcomes:* This specially tailored program will equip

131

Russian dairy trainers with the latest dairy management knowledge and extension training skills in the areas of agronomy, nutrition and feeding, reproduction and genetic selection, lactation and milking, raising dairy heifers, dairy farm business management.

· *Develop a training program for dairy farming workers and managers from Russia, including hands-on practical training at the farms in the United States.* Selected groups of Russian dairy workers and managers will be brought to the United States to complete four (4) months of on-farm training and two (2) weeks of intensive management technique training in a classroom setting.

· *Expected outcomes*: The participants will gain skills required to operate a successful and profitable dairy farm in positions such as: Agronomist; Nutrition and Feeding Technician; Custom Heifer Raising Technician; Dry Cow, Maternity, and Calf Raising Technician; Milking Technician; Reproduction and Genetic Selection Technician; Dairy Farm Business Manager.

· *Make dairy management software – Dairy Champ – available to trainers and trainees in the Russian language, fully adaptable to Russian dairy conditions.*

Expected outcomes: The software will have full operational capabilities and sufficient training capabilities with an extensive portfolio of help menus. The participants will be trained to use dairy management software and understand the operational reports which it generates.

· *Develop an on-going, on-site training program in Russia which is designed to disseminate the knowledge and experience gained at the first phase of the project.*

Expected outcomes: On-site extension classes will bring knowledge to the dairy farmers in Russia with an anticipated annual turnout of 100 attendees. At least two demonstration farms will provide practical learning opportunities for the interested Russian dairy farmers.

It is the intent of the participating partners to develop a joint proposal and seek funds from private sources, foundations, government agencies and international organizations to underwrite their collaborative effort.

The leadership for this program is provided by Dr. Richard Swanson, Director of International Agricultural Programs, Steven Clark, Associate Director and Jeffrey Reneau, Professor, Department of Animal Science at the University of Minnesota; Anatoly Duponen, Rector; Victor Storozhenko, Head Department of Foreign Studies; Yuri Isilov, Professor of Dairy Sciences, Timiryazev Agricultural Academy; and Ralph Hofstad, Andrei Danilenko and Andre Kravchenko, on behalf of RFCP's Dairy initiative.

See Appendix VII

BUSINESS DEVELOPMENT CENTER IS LAUNCHED

RFCP took a big step toward assuring the sustainability of its efforts in Russia when it established the Business Development Center (BDC) in late 1998.

The center, which was organized as a wholly owned subsidiary of the trust fund and RFCP was established for two primary reasons:

#1 To assist new and existing businesses in Russia to grow and become profitable, and

#2 To put in place a business entity which will be owned by RFCP's Russian staff when RFCP completes its involvement in Russia.

RFCP transferred its operating and administrative functions to BDC, including all personnel, equipment, furniture and vehicles. BDC will provide and charge for its services. All client services will be performed under standardized contracts and leases.

The Business Development Center is registered as a legal commercial enterprise in the city of Moscow. The trust fund provided the initial charter capital of 50 thousand rubles ($6,667).

The BDC provides a wide range of services to both foreign and Russian businesses such as management services, business plan development, feasibility and marketing studies, legal and accounting services and office services.

The BDC will assist new companies through their registration, start-up and growth phases to increase their chance of success.

In summary, RFCP transferred the commercial activities of its non-profit trust fund to a profitable business entity (BDC) which will offer needed services to clients at moderate prices, and provide meaningful employment and career opportunities for its Russian staff.

Andrei Danilenko served as the General Manager of BDC initially. In 1999 he named Alexei Domelov to that position. Further information about BDC can be found in Appendix VII.

See Appendix VIII

MAJOR DAIRY INITIATIVE IS LAUNCHED

In 1998, the Russian Farm Community Project (RFCP) committed itself to a major dairy initiative in the Dmitrov Raion which has far reaching implications for growing the economy of the region and meeting the basic milk needs of this region's people and, most especially, their children. RFCP organized a separate corporation, Russian Dairy Farms (RDF) to manage the dairy initiative. Planned over a period of three years, the Dairy Initiative is driven by a decline of 50% in milk production in the region over the past 7-8 years. Milk processing plants are operating at only 30-40 percent of their capacity and there is a critical and growing shortage of quality milk.

The dairy initiative will provide people in the Dmitrov Raion with management, technical, and financial assistance to establish new modern dairy facilities and new dairy herds which (over time) will be owned by the Russian dairy farmers.

Prior to launching the Dairy Initiative, RFCP asked John Vrieze, an outstanding Baldwin, Wisconsin dairy farmer and a member of the Board of Directors of the Russian Dairy Farms, Inc., to conduct an on site fact finding mission to assess the reasons for the poor output on Dmitrov region dairy farms. Skilled as both a dairyman and entrepreneur, the Baldwin dairy farmer represents three generations of family farming experience and leads the Midwest region in his transition to "state-of-the art" technology and management in dairy farming.

"We went in asking the big questions like – 'Do these Russian dairy cattle have the genetic potential required to produce more milk?' What we saw time and again was the urgent need to boost the nutritional value of the feed...the cows weren't preforming because of their diet," stated Vrieze.

It was a bit of good news in what was otherwise a bleak situation.

Across Russia, since 1990, total milk production has dropped by 34%; milk yield per cow has fallen 30%; and the dairy cattle population plunged 21%. Most Russian dairy enterprises teeter on the brink of bankruptcy. Significant changes are urgently needed in the whole chain from the feeding of the cattle to the processing and retailing of milk and milk products, according to Russian authorities. While producers are suffering, there is an enormous demand for quality raw milk to supply processors and the consumer.

Vrieze felt that three or four of the farms he visited could dramatically increase the amount of milk they produced with proper nutrition

135

management. "At the last dairy I visited, I was impressed not only with the high caliber of the herd's Dutch-American genetics but also with this farmer's attitude and work ethic. He was willing to learn and had a real hands on approach."

Turning around this farmer's nutritional problem could begin almost immediately, noted Vrieze.

"In 5 to 6 weeks, we could be helping him make progress by showing him a better way to mow, chop, and store his forages in bunker silo fashion," he continued. "The result? Better nutrition, and more milk from each cow."

> "We went in asking the questions...I was impressed...with this farmer's attitude and work ethic. He was willing to learn..."
>
> John Vrieze

On one farm he observed *"Deficiencies in the diets of your young stock will have a disastrous long term effect. Your adult cattle will never reach optimum size and therefore can never be expected to perform up to their genetic capabilities for milk production. Without proper diet, calves cannot grow into high producing adults thus leading to a downward spiral and diminishing returns."*

Consider the facts. On one farm Vrieze visited, the best of their 1,100 Ayrshire cows averaged about 10,474 pounds of milk annually. Compare that to the average of 25,000 pounds per cow on Vrieze's farm back in Wisconsin. At a Joint Stock Company dairy he visited, with 1,000 head of cows, the average dropped even lower – 7,169 pounds of milk per animal. A fourth farm visited on his tour was deemed a major money losing enterprise because of low milk production, poor genetics and general condition of the herd. Production was below 5,000 pounds of milk.

So where does RFCP begin to position Dmitrov as a model dairy land?

The RFCP dairy plan encompasses three goals. One: address the feed and nutrition situation; Two: improve the genetics; and Three: improve the dairy equipment/technology and herd management.

During the spring and summer of 2000 the Project established test plots to determine which crops could most quickly improve feed values in the region. Teaching and feeding demonstrations will also be stressed identifying sources of dietary requirements: protein, vitamins, and minerals.

RFCP's bottom line is that feed and nutritional problems must be addressed before it can be cost effective to improve the genetic bases of dairy cattle in the Dmitrov region.

The goal is to create significantly more income, more jobs and greater opportunities for the rural people of the Dmitrov Raion and most importantly, to provide more high quality, wholesome milk for the children in the region.

The ultimate goal is to double and even triple milk production per cow.

The first step in the Dairy Initiative was launched on May 6, 1999, at the Razdolye farm, a private family dairy farm owned by Nikolai and Julia Moskvin. The Moskvin family hosted representatives of the Administration of the Dmitrov Raion, the Russian Farm Community Project (RFCP), local private farmers, farm managers of large agricultural enterprises, and local and national media.

In the official ceremony Ralph Hofstad, RFCP Executive Director and Valery Gavrilov, Head of Administration of the Dmitrov Raion, announced the expansion of farm "Razdolye" from 50 to 140 dairy cows. In the symbolic ceremony Governor Gavrilov and Hofstad erected a pole which signified the site of the dairy barn that will house cows. A loan from RFCP made it possible for Moskvin to expand his herd of dairy cows from 50 to 140 cows with heifers shipped in from Holland. The loan also provided funding for the construction of a new free stall dairy barn and the necessary equipment. Ralph Hofstad and Andrei Danilenko, RFCP Country Director, presented the Governor with a ceramic cow and a symbolic check for sixty million dollars. The check signifies the potential investment funds that can be attracted into the Raion by the dairy initiative.

Russian Dairy Farms, Inc., a separate company established and owned by RFCP, has developed plans for a 60MM dollar dairy which has two phases: 1) a pilot operation, and 2) an extension phase. The first phase involves 1,600 cows. When the pilot operation meets the necessary standards for success, Phase Two will include an additional 12,000 cows on 12-20 farms.

John Vrieze, a very successful dairyman managing two Wisconsin dairy farms of 1,200 cows, directs and oversees this initiative. John's initial experiences in Russia go back to 1991 when he was selling Holstein embryos in Russia. During this period, he met a wonderful young Russian interpreter named Alona who today is his wife. Both Alona and John sit on the RFCP board.

John's leadership, knowledge and experiences in high-tech dairying, and his knowledge of Russian culture are invaluable to the success of the dairy initiative. He has had many visitors from Russia visit his farms in Wisconsin. He also understands that this is a community development project so neighbors to the new dairy operations will be given an opportunity to grow forages and other crops for the dairy farms and raise dairy heifer calves for them. When the dairy farms reach a point of profitability and all debts are fully manageable, they will be sold to local farmers at a modest and fair price.

In addition to Vrieze, RFCP's dairy initiative includes a three person team of Steve Bodart, Andre Kravchenko and possibly Michael Witty. Negotiations with Witty are in progress. Vrieze serves as the leader of the team and mentors and directs the dairy initiatives. Witty, if he accepts, will serve as the on-site manager of the dairy farms; Kravchenko is responsible for financing and overall coordination and Bodart is responsible for preparing business plans for each of the farms after Vrieze, Witty, and Kravchenko have agreed on the primary factors needed for success.

Vrieze, as already mentioned, is the owner/operator of two state-of-the-art 1,200 head dairy farms in Wisconsin and serves on the RFCP Board. Witty, is a former dairy farmer from Wisconsin and a livestock production specialist. He has extensive experience managing dairy farms in the U.S. and Russia, most recently in the former Soviet Republic of Kazakhstan.

Bodart, who has a Masters Degree in Animal Production from Iowa State University, was a Dairy Business Specialist at Land O'Lakes, Inc., one of the largest farmer-owned cooperatives in the United States, prior to joining Vrieze in his dairy operations in 1999.

Kravchenko, a native of the former Soviet Republic of Belarus, is a graduate of the Belarusian Sate Economic University, and has a degree in International Business. While in Belarus, he worked part-time at the Ministry of Foreign Economic Relations as Assistant to the Chief of Credit and Investments for the government of the Republic of Belarus. He also spent part of two years serving as the Business Development Manager of Orostrian Limited, a United Kingdom based construction and communication technologies company in Minsk, Belarus, and Moscow, Russia.

The Overseas Private Investment Corporation (OPIC), a private/public finance organization in Washington, D.C., has been approached to provide loans for the project. On September 29, 1999, OPIC issued a letter of commitment to Russian Dairy Farms, Inc. to provide an initial loan in the amount of $250,000 in support of the expansion project at the Razdolye farm. RDF is actively contacting other investors in preparing for the second and third phase of the dairy initiative which calls for two more 700 cow dairies.

On June 2, 1999,U.S. Ambassador to Russia, James Collins, visited the project site and commented "This truly represents a new beginning for agriculture in this region creating new sources of income, more jobs and greater opportunities for the people of the Dmitrov Raion, and equally important, more critically needed high quality wholesome milk for the children in the Region."

> "The RFCP dairy initiative truly represents a new beginning for agriculture in this region creating new sources of income, more jobs and greater opportunities for the people of the Dmitrov Raion and equally important more critically needed high quality wholesome milk for the children of the region."
>
> - The Honorable James Collins
> U.S. Ambassador to Russia

INTEGRATED DAIRY IMPROVEMENT PROJECT
"Russian Dairy Farms"

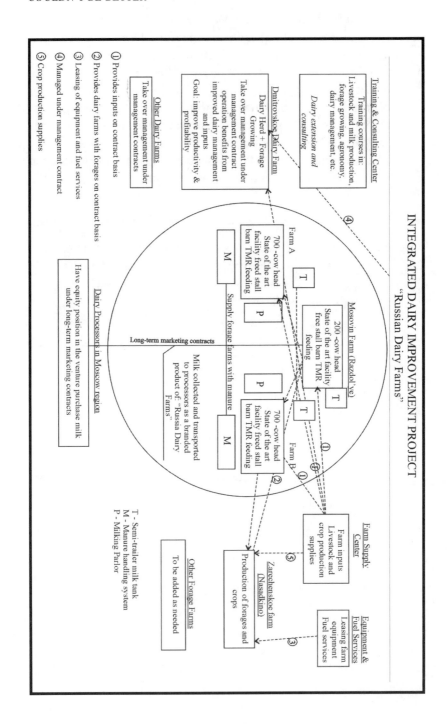

Training & Consulting Center

Dairy extension and consulting

Training courses in:
Livestock and milk production, forage growing, agronomy, dairy management, etc.

Dmitrovskoe Dairy Farm

Dairy Herd + Forage Growing

Take over management under management contract operation benefits from improved dairy management and inputs

Goal: improve productivity & profitability

Other Dairy Farms

Take over management under management contracts

① Provides inputs on contract basis

② Provides dairy farms with forages on contract basis

③ Leasing of equipment and fuel services

④ Managed under management contract

⑤ Crop production supplies

Farm A

700-cow head
State of the art facility freed stall barn TMR feeding

M   T   P

Mosovin Farm (Razdol'ye)

200-cow head
State of the art facility free stall barn TMR feeding

T

Supply forage farms with manure

Long-term marketing contracts

Farm B

700-cow head
State of the art facility freed stall barn TMR feeding

P   T   M

Milk collected and transported to processors as a branded product of: "Russia Dairy Farms"

Dairy Processors in Moscow region

Have equity position in the venture purchase milk under long-term marketing contracts

Farm Supply Center

Farm inputs
Livestock and crop production supplies

Zarechenskoe farm (Nasadkino)

Production of forages and crops

Equipment & Fuel Services

Leasing farm equipment
Fuel services

Other Forage Farms

To be added as needed

T - Semi-trailer milk tank
M - Manure handling system
P - Milking Parlor

FARM SUPPLY AND SERVICES CENTER

In 1999 RFCP contracted with Cooperative Business International (CBI) to establish a Farm Supplies and Services Center (FSSC) in the Dmitrov Raion to supply the dairy farms with feed and supplies.

While such a center is critically important long-term, it is currently on hold pending further study and funding.

In the interim, CBI will provide dairy feeding recommendations to the dairy farms, as well as any special ingredients, not grown locally, which are needed in the dairy rations to reach desired nutritional levels.

CBI also continues to study the best ways and means to supply the feed needs of the dairy farms.

PROCESSING AND DISTRIBUTION CENTER
BEGINS OPERATION

For a number of years one of Danilenko's and Hofstad's major objectives was to help the farmers in the Dmitrov Raion to build or acquire (and eventually own) a facility suitable for conversion into a potato and vegetable processing and distribution center. Such a center would clean, sort, and bag the farmers' produce and distribute and market them locally or in the huge Moscow market only 70 miles away.

Such a center would not only provide greater market opportunities for area farmers, but would be the catalyst for the development of a strong Farmers' Marketing Association.

The opportunity for such a facility presented itself when, after almost two years of negotiating, Danilenko and Hofstad and RFCP board member Richard Watts persuaded Yuri Luzhkov, the Mayor of Moscow, to transfer a bankrupt warehouse in Dmitrov to RFCP.

That was the first major breakthrough. The second was finding Al Vangelos, former President and CEO of Calavo, (an avocado cooperative in California), and convincing him to volunteer mentor the development of the Processing and Distribution Center.

Vangelos eagerly accepted the challenge and success was assured.

The center, which became operational in September of 1998, is a joint venture between RFCP and the Dmitrovsky Joint Stock Company (Dmitrovsky Farms) formerly the collective farm "Dmitrovsky" which was privatized in 1992. Dmitrovsky farms owns about 4,440 hectares of tillable land mainly used for growing potatoes, cabbage, carrots and beets.

RFCP provided "Dmitrovsky Farms Marketing Association" with a loan to pay for the renovation of the warehouse, and the equipment and supplies needed to launch the center.

Over a two year period, Vangelos advised and mentored the Russian management in the purchasing and installation of equipment; the planning and constructing of receiving and processing facilities, and the development and introduction of good business and management practices. He also helped them hire and train people including some of whom will work directly with farmers and market outlets.

Working with Hofstad, Danilenko, and the Russian staff, Vangelos helped the Russian farmers form their own marketing association to market their products in the Dmitrov Region, Moscow, and greater Russia.

Finally, Vangelos assisted the Russian staff in the development of a brand name, "Treasure of the Sun," for the products which are processed and distributed through the center.

At full capacity the center will be able to process 35-40 thousand tons of vegetables annually.

These products will be provided to the center by 30-50 farms in the area.

The center is exploring the feasibility of handling citrus, nuts, and other products that will be purchased in places like Hispain and Israel and delivered to the center by trucks.

The most exciting recent development is the possibility of constructing a potato chip plant on-site.

This will be accomplished through a five year contract with buyers looking for a reliable supply of high quality chips and a five year marketing contract with local potato growers looking for a reliable market for their potatoes.

Here is how Vangelos feels about the project and his mentoring efforts:

"Before the center was established, farmers would take their produce to Moscow in a burlap bag and get 25¢ on the dollar. Most produce buyers in Moscow looked to Holland which supplied 65% of the market with clean products and good packaging."

"Now the center provides a one-stop destination, where produce is cleaned, graded, sized and packaged – and then sold. In fact," Vangelos said, *"an agency in Moscow helped the distribution center come up with the first produce brand for a Russian product."*

Vangelos foresees even more ambitious growth in the future driven by such things as peeled potatoes, carrots and onions – a kind of precut borsht mix. In addition, another distribution facility may be built near the Black Sea — if an agreement between the Russian Farm Community Project and former Soviet leader Mikhail Gorbachev materializes.

Vangelos and others associated with the project have been able to contribute not only technical expertise but the principles of doing business as well.

"The biggest challenge is to change the mind-set of the people to more accountability and teamwork," he said, *"It has been a labor of love and has given me a real high."*

> My mentoring experiences have been a labor of love and have given me a real high.
>
> Allan Vangelos

RESTRUCTURING A BANKRUPT FORMER STATE FARM

Another major task undertaken by RFCP in 1999 involves the restructuring and bringing to profitability of a bankrupt privatized former state farm, the Zarechenskoe Joint Stock Company at Nasadkino.

The major players and their contributions are as follows:

- THE FARM itself which brings its agricultural production assets to the venture and shares in the net proceeds.
- RFCP which mentors the farms agricultural production and related activities, including the marketing of potatoes and vegetables through the new processing/distribution center.
- RFCP's INTERNATIONAL FUND IN MOSCOW which provides equity, and funding in the form of loans, which are repaid from net proceeds.
- THE DMITROV RAION whose Administration provides support in the form of approvals and guarantees under the Russian legal system.
- THE GOVERNOR of the Dmitrov Raion who has forgiven the historical debt on the farm.
- A NEW RUSSIAN MANAGEMENT TEAM, put in place by RFCP, which trains the employees.
- A CAPABLE FARM MANAGER, who has been hired to manage the farm.
- A NEW BOARD OF DIRECTORS which sets policy.

The goals of the venture are to:

- Develop a western style accounting system ("Scorecard") for all farms so they can see which enterprises are successful and which require special attention.
- Increase the yields and quality of agricultural crops.
- Achieve higher returns by marketing agricultural crops through the RFCP processing and distribution center.
- Develop efficient Human Resource management skills.
- Demonstrate how to bring a bankrupt former state farm to profitability through the use of good management practices relating to production, financing, marketing, and personnel.

THE GOAL IS TO MAKE THE FARM PROFITABLE IN TWO YEARS.

COMMUNITY INITIATIVES EXPANDED

Since the beginning of its efforts in Russia, RFCP's over-riding principle has been to pursue a holistic approach in its development initiatives, wherever possible serving the needs of the broader community in which its agricultural initiatives are focused.

Through the years, this has led RFCP to address such needs as dental care, youth programs, social services, health and medical care.

As those needs became apparent, RFCP's approach had been to identify people in the U.S. with the passion and skills to address such needs, assist them in soliciting the needed funds and supplies to meet those needs, and provide them with administrative support. Often such people have come forward to volunteer their services before they were asked.

The first of those people was Susan Dudas who along with Ludmilla Burch, provided the leadership for the development of a dental clinic; computer and English classes, a cottage industry in sewing, and the youth program Teens Uniting Globally (TUG) which are noted earlier in this book.

More recently Dr. Norm Broadbent, Pastor of the Falcon Heights, Minnesota, United Church of Christ, Dr. Norman Westhoff, M.D. in Occupational Health in Roseville, Minnesota and Doug Aretz, Administrator of an elder care center in St. Cloud, Minnesota, have stepped forward to provide the leadership and mentoring for Youth, Health, and Social Services programs.

Dr. Broadbent's initiatives in the youth area are presented in the next section of this book. Suffice to say, his leadership and the youth programs are closely entwined with the health and social services initiative.

None of these initiatives would be possible without the support and assistance of Governor Gavrilov and his associates in the Dmitrov Raion and the many other people in the United States who have provided countless hours of time and effort.

Russians who deserve special praise and thanks for these efforts are Galina Zveva, Deputy for Youth Services; Alla Pospelova, Deputy for Health Services; and Elena Vinogradova, Deputy for Social Services and Education on Governor Gavrilov's staff.

In early 1998 Norm Westhoff and Doug Aretz made an assessment trip to the Dmitrov Raion and joined with Russian health officials to determine healthcare and social service needs.

They identified six areas of immediate need:
Medical/Hospital Equipment, Medical Supplies and Drugs,
Health Education Programs,
Health Care Professionals Exchanges,
Transitional Shelters for the Elderly,
Transportation for the Disabled, and
A Healthcare/Social Services Endowment.

To meet the needs for medical/hospital equipment, medical supplies and drugs, RFCP is using its network and partnerships to send used medical and hospital equipment and disposable supplies to the Dmitrov Raion.

Three cargo containers of donated durable hospital equipment were successfully shipped and distributed to Dmitrov hospitals in the fall of 1998. Shipping was funded and arranged through Counterpart International, Washington, D.C., through which RFCP is now authorized to make such shipments. This network is being used to send hospital equipment and disposable medical supplies, for which there is an ongoing source in the Twin Cities. They are assembled by Minneapolis/St. Paul Roteract Clubs and stored in a warehouse maintained by the Midway Rotary Club of St. Paul.

Drug Donations

The Oncology Department at the Dmitrov Hospital has requested a large quantity of drugs used in the treatment of cancer as well as other drugs. A pipeline has been established to route the drugs from participating manufacturers to a relief agency and then to RFCP in Dmitrov. RFCP is also asking U.S. mentors to take quantities of drugs with them when they travel to Dmitrov. This piggyback schedule allows for a shipment every 2-3 months. Such a schedule is necessary because typically, donated drugs have a six-month expiration date, or shelf life. Also, Russian Customs' rules limit the value of each humanitarian donation to $10,000.

Custom clearance for drugs needs to be worked out in advance, and is much more difficult than in the case of durable equipment.

Oncology drugs usually aren't requested for international relief programs, and therefore, manufacturers and relief agencies are less prepared to deal with these requests. Antibiotics and other acute care drugs are more readily available for donations.

RFCP's health education initiatives in the Dmitrov Raion are focusing on Preventive Health Care — heart disease; prenatal care, family planning, and health professional education programs.

Preventive Health Care – Heart Disease

Heart disease is the #1 cause of death in Russia. And there is a great need to improve health conditions and treatment practices ranging from primary care to secondary preventative methods, to tertiary prevention. It will require more and better public health education and a long-term commitment by those involved in health education.

The Dmitrov Administration has identified an interested health professional ("champion") who will take a leadership role in providing public health education, and addressing other preventative issues. That "champion" will spend time in the U.S. familiarizing himself with the materials and practices needed to implement a preventive health care program.

Prenatal Care and Family Planning – 85-90% of pregnant women in the Dmitrov Raion experience complications. Nearly 85% are hospitalized early in their third trimester. The birth defect rate is perceived to be high, and the overall birth rate has declined from an average of 2 to 1.2 births per family over recent years.

RFCP will assist in a research program to determine the following:

· How many of the infant deaths and defects are due to prenatal causes?

· How many of these deaths and defects are due to prenatal malnutrition, lack of vitamins, and/or drug and alcohol use?

· How much is due to prenatal infections, some of which may be traceable to food or water pollution sources. The high rate of pediatric hospital admissions for gastroenteritis suggests contaminated food and/or water sources. This study will require the cooperation of the Sanitation Ministry, which is administered entirely separately from the Health Ministry.

· The study will attempt to determine the number of deaths and defects caused by water and/or air pollution, and/or heavy metals, benzene, chlorinated hydrocarbons, or other industrial chemicals. This study will require the cooperation of local industries and whichever authority is responsible for environmental protection.

147

In addition to assisting with the research program, RFCP is collaborating in the preparation of prenatal education materials, a prenatal vitamin packet program, a pilot program in providing bottled water for pregnant women, and an environmental protection assessment program in the Dmitrov Raion.

Health Care Professionals Exchanges

The purpose of this initiative is to identify ways and means for establishing more effective and continuing connections between US and Russian health professionals and among health professionals in the Dmitrov Raion to assure appropriate health education and methodology for the people who live in the Dmitrov Raion

The goal is to organize programs and opportunities for a physicians' exchange, whereby, American physicians travel to Dmitrov, visit medical facilities, and meet and work with their counterpart Russian physicians and Russian physicians visit medical facilities and their American counterparts in Minnesota.

The first of such exchanges took place in 2000 under the leadership of Dr. Westhoff, and consisted of physicians from Minnesota going to Russia.

The American physicians, paid their own airfare, and were lodged at the RFCP guest house in Ramenýe. A group of Dmitrov physicians from various specialities will visit medical facilities in the Twin Cities in 2001. This will be especially beneficial to the primary care health providers, whose skill is less dependent on expensive technology. The goal is to improve and expand the delivery of outpatient, clinic-based health care.

In the social services area, championed by Doug Aretz, the goal is the construction of a transitional facility for the elderly and more adequate transportation for the disabled in the Dmitrov Raion.

Transitional Shelter for the Elderly

The construction of a transitional shelter for the elderly in Dmitrov will provide medical and social services to elderly people who are unable to care for themselves and/or need some assistance.

The plan is to construct a 24 unit facility adjacent to an existing day-program facility.

Such a facility is needed to meet the needs of a growing number of elderly people (women, older than 55 years' men, older than 60 years): This number has grown from 11.8% of the population in 1959 to 20.5% of the population in 1996.

The number of people aged 85 and older has increased by more than three fold since 1959.

In the Dmitrov Raion, Moscow Oblast, the number of retired people is about 44,000, or 29% of the population.

An analysis of the of elderly population, found the following problems to be prevalent among the elderly people in Russia.

- Poor health – Elderly people get sick six times more often than younger people; up to 80% of elderly people need medical – social help; more than 70% of them have 4-5 chronic diseases.
- Poverty – The main source of income for the majority of the elderly people in Russia is their pension. In 1996 pension payments made up about 37% of the average person's income. As a result a considerable number of elderly people are living below the poverty level.
- Need – accessibility designed buildings to accommodate elderly and handicapped persons are presently not available in the Dmitrov Raion. Such a facility will provide immediate assistance for the elderly, and will demonstrate why such a facility is so important to their well-being.

Transportation for the Disabled

The plan is to provide a handicapped accessible vehicle (van) with a mechanical lift for transporting people with disabilities to health care facilities and other places they need to go.

Currently there are no such vehicles available which are specially designed to transport such people.

- The Dmitrov Raion Administration will be responsible for the maintenance of the handicapped accessible van; develop a plan for its use, and identify the type of vehicle they could maintain from a mechanical standpoint.
- The Russian Farm Community Project will provide most of the funding through private contributors.

See Appendix IX

YOUTH PROGRAM EXPANDS AND FLOURISHES

In 1998 Dr. Norman Broadbent, Pastor of the United Church of Christ in Falcon Heights, Minnesota and a member of the RFCP Board of Directors, took over the mentorship of RFCP's Teens Uniting Globally (TUG) program that was founded by Susan Dudas in 1995.

Exhibiting the same traits of energy, passion and creativity as Susan, he expanded and developed the program even further.

In its first years, under Susan's leadership, the program had involved American teens going to Russia and joining with Russian youth in specified work projects.

Broadbent retained that dimension and added two more. One of those dimensions is called the Reverse TUG program or TUGR, and involves bringing Dmitrov youth to the United States to receive specialized training in peer helping; alcohol, drug, and suicide education/prevention; and volunteerism.

The other dimension which was launched in 2000 is called YAARN (Young Adult American/Russian Network) and involves young adults from the two countries also joining together in community service-based projects in the Dmitrov region. The first pilot project for YAARN is the renovating of the "House of Kindness" facility in Dmitrov which provides daycare for elderly persons in the Raion.

The purpose of the TUG program is to provide an opportunity for 10-14 American teenagers and adult advisors to go to Russia for a period of 10 days annually to join with Russian youth and advisors on a community service project selected by Russian community leaders.

The purpose is:

·   To provide an opportunity for American and Russian youth to get to know each other and build friendships by working together on projects which will benefit the community in which those projects are carried out.

·   To provide American youth with the opportunity to experience some of Russia and its culture and Russian youth an opportunity to experience American youth.

The staff of the Russian Farm Community Project in the U.S. and Russian members of the Dmitrov Youth Council plan and operate the program.

· ·   U.S. youth and/or their sponsors pay a $2,500 fee to cover costs.

·   Adult advisors pay a $1,250 fee

·   RFCP pays half the cost, $1,250 for each adult advisor

·   The Dmitrov Youth Council covers the rest of the costs.

The TUGR program brings up to seven Russian teens (chosen by the Dmitrov Youth Council) and two adult advisors, to the United States for 10 days to receive mentoring and training in three specific areas: crisis intervention, peer counseling, and emergency shelter services for teens.

The TUGR program grew out of a need identified by U.S. medical and health officials who traveled to the Dmitrov Raion as part of RFCP's community needs assessment effort in 1998. During their visit they identified a critical need for dealing with alcoholism and drug addictions among youth; especially identified was a growing population of homeless youth. The Dmitrov Raion requested American assistance to deal with their problems and suggested training for Russian youth in crisis intervention, peer counseling, and the operation of an emergency shelters for youth, perhaps in conjunction with a TUG project during the summer.

Rather than trying to educate/mentor the Russian teens in a relative vacuum of experience and resources, Dr. Norman Westhoff (leader of the medical professionals) proposed bringing a contingent of Dmitrov youth and advisors to Minneapolis/St. Paul where they would have access and support from several important resources: the Hazelden Center, the Mayors' Commission Against Drugs (MCAD), Project Solo (transient street youth), The Bridge (shelter and counseling for street teens) and the Augsburg Peer Ministry Training Program, to name a few. MCAD, which coordinates much of the drug/alcohol compliance programs in Roseville (Ramsey County), Minnesota, provided mentoring sessions and demonstration projects for the Russian delegation. A grant from the United Church of Christ Board for World Ministries was used to help underwrite this first highly successful TUGR initiative.

The St. Anthony Park United Church of Christ in Minnesota coordinated the housing and hospitality activities during their entire stay. Aaron and Carrie Roberts, two adult advisors for the 1998 TUG Program, provided overall leadership. Five Minnesota participants in the 1998 TUG program scheduled social events and a "reunion" for the Russian and American youth. The Falcon Heights United Church of Christ arranged a Habitat of Humanity project, so there would be a "helping in reverse" experience for the Russian and American youth.

This program costs approximately $20,000 annually and is entirely funded by donations from U.S. contributors and the Dmitrov Duma. The impact of this TUGR experience was apparent in the follow-up

151

efforts of the Dmitrov group. Within weeks after their return to Russia they made a presentation to Governor V.V. Gavrilov and formulated a plan to give the same presentation in each junior high school in the raion to recruit and train other peer helpers. A delegation from the youth Council also traveled to Moscow to tour alcohol and drug rehabilitation facilities. Fueled by the initiative of the Dmitrov youth, professionals from those programs now come to Dmitrov on a regular basis to assist in intervention activities and educational programs for the youth. The governor was so impressed with the work of the Russian youth that he has included them in his youth Council.

The YAARN program provides opportunities for young American adults, 20-30 years old, to join Russian young adults of similar ages in community work projects in the Dmitrov Raion.

The program is funded by the participants, RFCP and the administration of the Dmitrov Raion, and provides a first-hand opportunity for American and Russian young adults to get to know each other, develop friendships and work together for a common cause — "helping people to move forward after the collapse of Communism."

In the process, both Americans and Russians learn the value of cooperation and volunteerism.

Here is how Dr. Broadbent described the 1999 TUG program in Russia:

"Our purpose for going to Russia was twofold: first, to immerse ourselves in a people-to-people experience, appreciating Russian culture, history, religious traditions, and family values; second, to purposefully work with our hands in cooperation with Russian youth in building something tangible and meaningful, a symbol of the spirit of cooperation and understanding which our Christian faith asks of us. Throughout the experience, we were to ask ourselves on a daily basis, "Where today have I seen the face of Christ." That became the focal point for each evening's reflection, prayer, and meditation.

We saw the face of Christ in the company of Russian Protestant Christians quietly and effectively seeking to enflesh the gospel through an outreach to young people in Dmitrov. We saw the face of Christ in the faces of those who made us feel so welcome, and called us 'brothers and sisters in Christ.'

But that aside, it was to build a fence that we had come to Nasadkino. This project was selected because a fence around a hockey /soccer field could be a major recreational center for an otherwise depressed region. It would stand as a symbol that there was a future, that economic and social recovery was possible. It was to be a place for the young.

Our high expectations for completing the project, were diminished somewhat when we arrived to find no tools and no supplies awaiting us. Remaining old stringers to a decades old decaying former fence had not been removed; bolts and nuts were rusted into place. How to even get started without the basic tools such as wrenches and pliers? But the combined resourcefulness and ingenuity of both American and Russian youth took over. A power saw was borrowed from a neighboring work site, and old stringers were sawed away (until the saw ran out of gasoline). Two sets of metric wrenches appeared and two teams began to grunt and tug away at rusted bolts. A hatchet appeared from a villager, and shortly several began chipping away at stringer stubs holding old rusted bolts and bolts, as well as at remaining stringers. A gentleman from the village, Lief, showed up with a small water bottle filled with gasoline, and gestured that dribbling gasoline on the rusted bolts might loosen the nut enough for us to undo it. Two other men from the village showed up with a portable acetylene torch and worked on the rusted nuts and bolts (the non-gasoline ones!) Old stringers were carted away to begin a wood pile; our teams of young people hard at work, but joined by children of the village.

At the nearby community center a stereo system and public address system was set up, and contemporary Russian "techno rock" was played for our "enjoyment!" In between CD's, a man from the village took his accordion and, standing near the microphone, played for us Russian folk songs and dances. As the fence began to take shape, larger clusters of villagers began to appear. Children were ever-present, eager to help, let alone look and gaze at this wonderful thing that was taking shape in their village.

We would need to finish our work by 6:00 p.m., as that is when our bus transport was going to arrive to return us to our quarters and an evening meal in Novasinkova. By two p.m. we began to hear new voices, children's voices singing over the loudspeaker. There seemed to be a noticeable increase in energy, in activity, and in expectation. By 5 p.m., the very last nails of the very last boards were driven in a "last board ceremony." Alternating between Russian and American youth, the fence was completed! Simultaneously, a children's soccer game spontaneously started, with several American youth joining in. By 5:15 p.m. we were being summoned to the community center, as the children of the village proceeded to entertain us all with singing, danc-

ing, and games. We were all invited to join in the celebration, which culminated in a tug 'o war between the men/boys and women/girls. The latter won!

It is hard to describe the sense of accomplishment, of teamwork, of partnership that came out of that day. The villagers told us they didn't believe the project would be finished. History tells them that lots of things get started, but very seldom are finished. And imagine, American youth coming to work with their hands! Imagine, Russian youth sharing in such labor! Imagine! It is a miracle!

And so it was that the face of Christ was made manifest in Nasadkino, enfleshed in a community of youth, villagers, and children. The Realm of God made visible again by wood and nails. Ironic and spiritually overwhelming.

As we gathered that night for our evening's reflection and prayer, the Russian young people were invited to join us for the first time in our devotions. Thirty of us crammed onto three beds of a dormitory room to again reflect on the questions we had brought with us. We went person-by-person, encouraging a word, a reflection, a hope from each one there. Everyone had some grateful word, observation, hope to offer. But it was Mikhail from Dmitrov who perhaps summed things up most poignantly when he observed, "In most times and places a fence is built to keep people apart, to separate them according to politics, or economics, or religion. I look at the fence we built and can only think of how it has brought us together! This fence is different, because we made it different." — with the help of God."

How important is the TUG program? Here is what some of the other participants said. <u>In their own words</u>.

Dima Koifmann, president of the Dmitrov Youth Duma: *"This experience is like going into a library room and finding a book that you've always wanted to read. The writing is superb, the characters make you fall in love with them, the story pulls you along so that you can't put the book down. Now, as you notice that there are but a few pages left until the book ends, you start to read more and more slowly, because you just don't want it to end."*

Christine Wilkes of Garden Grove, California: *"I came to Russia expecting to learn something more about God...I have experienced so much more. A part of me wishes God hadn't made the world so* *big, because now I'm going to be so far from people I have come to love."*

Aaron Watts, Fullerton, California: *"The TUG program is definitely the most heartwarming experience I have ever had. I have already promised myself that someday I will return to look into the faces of the children I have come to love."*

Daniel Hofstad, Minneapolis, Minnesota: *"The TUG experience is very unique and unlike any other experience I have ever had. It is my goal to see that the TUG program continues and does not fade into the memories of the past."*

Thanks to outstanding leadership, participants and support from both the U.S. and Russia side, the TUG program and its offshoots, TUGR and YAARN, have been very successful and have truly made a difference and the best is yet to come.

In the summer of 2000 Broadbent took a three month leave of absence from his church to go to Dmitrov and work with his Russian counterparts to assure that the Seeds of Hope and promise which have been planted through RFCP's youth programs will continue to grow and flourish even after RFCP is no longer involved.

155

A CHURCH FOR RAMENÝE

One of the most significant and tangible initiatives undertaken by RFCP in the Dmitrov Raion was the conversion of an elementary school into a training and education center for teaching people about the private enterprise system.

You may recall the school was described as standing literally in the shadow of St. Matthew's church, a Russian Orthodox Church, which during the Communist regime had served first as a grainery and later as a sports center.

Called the "Stone" church in Ramenýe, it began as a wooden church and dates back to the 17th Century when it began as the property of one of Russia's wealthiest monasteries, Medvedeva Pustyn.

The church has served the people in Ramenýe and its surrounding community since the 17th Century except for the 74 year period of Communist rule, when as stated earlier, it was first used as a grainery and later as a sports facility.

In 1842 the wooden church was replaced by a stone church in commemoration of the 30th anniversary of victory during the 1812 Patriotic War.

The church reopened in 1991 but minus the bells in the church steeple which had been removed by the Communists and melted for iron. Its years as a grainery and sports facility have taken its toll and the church is in critical need of repair and renovation. Since the church is an architectural masterpiece the renovation will include some complex and costly restoration.

The Dmitrov Administration, the church members, and the community began reconstruction of the church in 1991, but progress has been slow.

In 1997 V.V. Gavrilov, Chief Administrator of the Dmitrov region and R.R. Rome, Senior Church Official for the Dmitrov region, asked RFCP if it would participate in the revival of the cultural and spiritual heritage of the Dmitrov Raion by providing some funds for the church renovation/restoration project.

Given its own Christian roots, Churches Uniting in Global Mission, and the significance of this church to RFCP beginnings in the Dmitrov Raion, RFCP responded with an enthusiastic yes and is in the process of raising funds to cover one third of the renovation costs or approximately $55,000.

MIKHAIL GORBACHEV ENTERS THE PICTURE

For a number of years there were indications that the former (and last) president of the Soviet Union, Mikhail Gorbachev, was becoming increasingly more aware of RFCP's efforts in the Dmitrov Raion to the point that he was interested in meeting Hofstad and Danilenko to discuss the possibility of RFCP establishing a similar model agricultural development project in his home area near Stavropol in Southern Russia.

Such a meeting was arranged in the early fall of 1998 and included Dr. Otis Young, Chair of the RFCP board, Dr. Ronald Roskens, RFCP board member from Omaha, Nebraska and their wives, in addition to Hofstad and Danilenko.

Roskens described the meeting as enlightening and instructive. "After introductions, in which we all referenced our rural backgrounds, Gorbachev indicated that he could really identify with us since his father and grandfather, and he himself, were all peasants and thus we could commence our discussion with agrarian solidarity. "We spent nearly an hour engaged in a lively discussion with Mr. Gorbachev."

Gorbachev expressed keen interest in the work of RFCP, and it was clear early on that he understood the nature of RFCP's undertaking stating that he was especially appreciative of RFCP's efforts to enable former collective farmers to strike out on their own initiative and felt, among other things, we were teaching them responsibility. He also stated, "that while he was supportive of our project, he could become even more enthusiastic if we implemented similar plans in his home area. We offered to take it under advisement."

Dr. Young asked Gorbachev his opinion about current happenings in Russia and he observed that it was both sensible and necessary that President Clinton had made the trip to Moscow a couple of days earlier. Even though both President Clinton and Yeltsin are "lame ducks" he felt that if Clinton had canceled, it would have sent the wrong message in Russia. With respect to the current political and economic dilemmas, he made it clear that President Yeltsin should resign and call for new elections. He agreed there are no easy answers, but the problems needed to be faced immediately. Overall, he felt that Russia had attempted to move from Communism to Capitalism much too quickly without the necessary knowledge, infrastructure and government support.

Gorbachev's open and relaxed manner made the session memorable and enjoyable.

157

Subsequent meetings involving Gorbachev, Hofstad, and Danilenko, and Danilenko and Gorbachev's staff, culminated in the signing of a Memorandum of Agreement and a tentative commitment to explore the establishment of a model project in Gorbachev's home area after the Dmitrov model reaches Sustainability in the year 2001 or 2002.

In return, Gorbachev committed to visiting the United States and assisting in the raising of funds for such a project.

See Appendix X

THEY GIVE FROM THEIR HEARTS

Many people believe that funding economic development efforts in foreign countries is the responsibility of government and to a great extent that is true.

But there are others, equally passionate, who believe that private citizens have a responsibility and opportunity as well, to become involved, to make a difference, and to help those less fortunate than they to put themselves in a position to succeed and to become active players in their societies.

It is to the latter segment of our society that RFCP has directed its appeal for contributions in support of its initiatives; and they have responded in a manner that has generated over $350,000 in private contributions annually.

The board members set the standard by contributing $2,500 or more annually ($1,000 annually for clergy members). Executive Director Hofstad set the bar even higher and the people have responded — individuals, churches, corporations, organizations and foundations. The contributions have been given in the form of cash, checks, stock, equipment and supplies.

Some groups of interested persons, including Susan Dudas and Beth Godard organized Circles of Support to access funding for RFCP, to provide feedback to the staff and leaders of RFCP, and assist in recruiting volunteers and organizing tours.

Solicitation has also been by way of RFCP's quarterly newsletter, direct mail, personal calls, tours, and meetings.

These contributions have helped RFCP make a difference for people and areas for which public funds have not been readily available, such as youth, health and dental care, and the elderly.

Private contributors have provided "Seeds of Hope" from which world peace and stability can grow.

The motto from the beginning has been "No gift is to large or small and new contributions are always welcome."

> They have provided "Seeds of Hope" from which world peace and stability can grow.

The Honorable Yuri Luzhkov, Mayor of
Moscow, stands with Danilenko, Hofstad, and
Richard Watts, Vice Chair of the RFCP board
after he transferred a bankrupt processing plant
facility to RFCP.

Hofstad and Danilenko "sealing" the joint
venture agreement for the processing and
distribution center with Fedor Azorkin, head of
Dmitrovsky Joint Stock Company.

Grading, sizing and cleaning potatoes before
packaging at the processing and distribution center.

RFCP Russian employees, Constantine Kravtsov and Muslim Umiryaev, with freshly bagged potatoes.

Allan Vangelos, Chief RFCP mentor and advisor
for the processing and distribution center, and
Andrei Danilenko, hold a bag of potatoes right
off the assembly line.

The new trademark "Treasure of the Sun."

Hofstad, Gavrilov, Vern Moore, Alexei Mikeev, and former TUGR participants at signing of the social program agreement.

All signed, Gavrilov presents agreement to Hofstad.

L-R – Galina Zveva, Deputy for Youth Services, Alla Pospelova, Deputy for Health Services, and Elena Vinogradova, Deputy for Social Services and Education in the Dmitrov Raion, pose with Vern Moore, RFCP staff member and Head of Social Programs for RFCP.

1999 TUGR participants who participated in the social services program agreement signing.

The "Island of Hope" teen facility with the
newly built hockey arena in the foreground.

Eugeny Semenov, the first ever director of the
Island of Hope teen center in Dmitrov.

Russian teenagers, Yulia Azorkina, Alexei Miheev, and Marina Vinogradova with their chaperone, Galina Zveva, prepare to serve meals to the needy in a day care center in St. Paul, Minnesota.

The Reverend Dr. Norman Broadbent, chief mentor for the TUG and TUGR programs for RFCP, front center, surrounded by American and Russian youth who were part of the 1998 TUG program.

Dr. Ronald Roskens, RFCP board member (third from
left) and Ralph Hofstad (far right) meet with Mikhail
Gorbachev (Dr. Otis Young, RFCP board chair was also
at this meeting).

Gorbachev hears about the processing and
distribution center from Allan Vangelos.

Gavrilov, Hofstad, and board chair Otis Young,
meet with Russian Ambassador to the U.S., Yuri
Varestosov (second from right), at the Russian
Embassy in Washington, D.C.

Dr. Broadbent with members of the Dmitrov
Raion Youth Council.

Members of the RFCP board and staff
Rear L-R: Vern Moore, Ronald Roskens, Larry
Buegler, John Cotton, Ron Hofstad, Richard Watts,
Otis Young, Norm Broadbent, Alona Vrieze, David
Tyler Scoates, and Priscilla Whitehead

Front L-R: John Vrieze, Ralph Hofstad, Vern Freeh,
Andre Danilenko, J.T. Scott

ASSESSING THE FUTURE

Russia is at a point where it needs to seriously take stock of where it is, where it eventually wants to be, and what it needs to do to get there.

When privatization was launched most Russians, and most foreigners wishing to do business in Russia, had no idea how awesome a task that would be.

Gorbachev had it right when he said recently that Russia's problem was that it tried to move from Communism to Capitalism to quickly without the necessary knowledge, infrastructure, and government support.

Moreover, many of the people in leadership positions at the time were selfish and uncaring about the needs and aspirations of the masses.

Far too few were "invited to the table" when privatization was launched and the oligarches and bankers were given far too many opportunities to receive the best deals and to accumulate wealth.

If privatization and democratization are to succeed, things will have to change rather dramatically and rapidly.

The things that have been missing to this point need to be put into place without returning to centralized government control.

People need to be educated in the ways of private enterprise and supported by the government as they find their way. Appropriate policies and an infrastructure need to be put into place to support private initiatives, and "scorecards" need to be created for measuring success in all segments of society. Those scorecards need to be at least as good as those which already exist in the areas of space, military, and sports.

This will not be easy and will require time, strong government support, and effective partnering with countries like the United States that already have in place the types of policies, infrastructure, government support, scorecards, and business climate that are essential for a vital and vibrant democracy.

Participating countries will benefit from such partnerships as long as each is willing to give as much as they get from the partnership.

Russia's economic difficulties have actually created opportunities for RFCP initiatives. Imports of agricultural goods have decreased because they are no longer affordable for the vast majority of the population. As a result, the demand for domestic farm products is accelerating and needs to be met by enterprising farmers like those RFCP is assisting.

In order for Russia's economy to develop, there needs to be a **solid** base of production — the very area in which RFCP is focusing its efforts.

The support of the U.S. and Russian governments is critical to RFCP's success.

Unfortunately, that support, in the form of monetizable commodities, has not been forthcoming from the U.S. government since 1998.

For various reasons, not entirely clear, (but supposedly having to do with monetization problems experienced by several U.S. private voluntary organizations, as well as deeper political issues), the U.S. government has temporarily discontinued the practice of providing monetizable commodities to organizations such as RFCP for economic development work in Russia.

Instead, in both 1999 and 2000 they restricted their efforts in Russia to direct food assistance programs on a government-to-government basis.

This is most unfair to RFCP which has been successful in its economic development initiatives. Moreover, it leaves RFCP's programs in limbo and in jeopardy — two years from sustainability.

After six years of building trust, confidence, and good feelings with the Russian people, and programs which have won the plaudits of U.S. and Russian government officials, RFCP is put in the position of possibly having to curtail its efforts and abandon its successful and expanding economic development initiatives. Not a nice way to treat friends or to end a relationship.

Needless to say, Hofstad and members of the RFCP board and staff have made their plight known to key congressional and government agency leaders and the White House. The hope is that the government will again provide RFCP with the monetizable commodities it needs to achieve sustainability for its initiatives, but currently there is no assurance that it will happen.

Russia is a unique country, with some of the world's most highly educated people and most abundant natural resources.

Its greatest needs are good leadership, sound policies, adequate financing and a government and infrastructure which supports private initiatives.

If they succeed in putting it all together, everyone will benefit – not only in Russia, but throughout the world.

RFCP's goal, as it has been from the beginning, is to help rural Russian people achieve a better quality of life and a more productive economy through the use of improved agricultural practices and a more efficient and more profitable food and agricultural system. All this while heeding the advice of Mikhail Gorbachev and others who have said, " In providing your assistance, please remember to respect our history, our culture, our governmental structure, and the need for our people to ultimately provide the initiative, vision, and hard work for doing what needs to be done."

RFCP is proud of its accomplishment in Russia and deeply grateful to all who have partnered, assisted, and contributed – public and private.

RFCP is hopeful that it can continue to provide assistance to the Russian people until they are firmly launched on the road to democratization and free enterprise initiatives.

That's the need, the opportunity, and the challenge.

THE SEEDS OF HOPE ARE SPROUTING

On April 14, 2000, Danilenko and Hofstad received the following letter, indicating that the "Seeds of Hope" RFCP has planted are beginning to sprout.

JOINT-STOCK COMMERCIAL BANK FOR
AGRICULTURE, INDUSTRY &
CONSTRUCTION
"AGROPROMSTROYBANK"

Head Office: 16, Krasina Lane
Moscow, 123056, Russia
Telex: 709965 AGBNK
Fax: (07 095)254-70-81
Tel: (07 095)254-42-63
Date: 14.04.2000

To: Mr. Ralph Hofstad   Mr. Andrei Danilenko
Chairman, Trust Fund "Russian Farms"   President, Trust Fund "Russian Farms"
Executive Director, Russian Farm   Russia Director, Russian Farm
Community Project   Community Project
Minneapolis, Minnesota USA   Moscow, Russia

Dear Mr. Hofstad and Mr. Danilenko:

We have the pleasure to inform you that we have reviewed the Russian Farm Community Project program and your progress in the Dmitrov Region, and that we support the objectives of the project and the need for additional funding for the next two years to achieve sustainability. This program can be replicated throughout Russia.

In this respect, AGROPROMSTROYBANK is willing to match $10 million dollars of special US legislative funding, if approved by Congress. This match could take the form of an equity investment or that of a loan.

We welcome this opportunity and assure you of our continued support to the Russian Farm Community Project.

Yours faithfully,

Victor Vidmanov
Chairman of the Board

EPILOGUE

If Russia succeeds in its democratization efforts, much of the credit needs to go to people like Andrei Danilenko.

Young, highly intelligent, dedicated, and articulate, this outstanding young man has performed in a most exceptional manner at the front lines of RFCP initiatives.

He has set a standard for all in his generation and his country to emulate.

APPENDICES

APPENDIX I
REFERENCE PAGE

General Council Churches Uniting In Global Mission

· LeRoy Bailey
First Baptist Church
Hartford, Connecticut

· Don Benton
Lovers Lane Methodist
Dallas, Texas

· William Brokett
International Christian
Staten Island, New York

· Fulton Buntain
First Assembly of God
Tacoma, Washington

· John Calhoun
First Church of the Nazarene
Long Beach, California

· Gabe Campbell
First Congregational Church
Akron, Ohio

· James Capps
Bonhomee Presbyterian Church
Chesterfield, Maryland

· Ray Cotton
Central Community
Wichita, Kansas

· Roger Douglas
St. Phillips in the Hills
Tuscan, Arizona

· Howard Edington
First Presbyterian
Orlando, Florida

· Buckner Fanning
Trinity Baptist
San Antonio, Texas

· Dale Galloway
New Hope Community
Portland, Oregon

· David Galloway
Christ's Episcopal Church
Tyler, Texas

· L.H. Hardwick
Christ Church
Nashville, Tennessee

· Daryl Higgins
First Protestant Church
New Braunfels, Texas

· William Hinson
First Methodist
Houston, Texas

· H. Stuart Irvin
All Saints Episcopal
Chevy Chase, Maryland

· Walt Kallestad
Community Church of Joy
Glendale, Arizona

· Randolph Kowalski
First Presbyterian
Greenville, South Carolina

· Bruce Larson
Crystal Cathedral
Garden Grove, California

· Robert Lawrence
First Congregational
Fall River, Massachusetts

· Daniel Matthews
Trinity Church
New York, New York

· Jess Moody
Shepard of the Hills
Porter Ranch, California

· Don Morgan
First Church of Christ
Wethersfield, Connecticut

176

- John Myers
Clay United Methodist
South Bend, Indiana

- Maynard Nelson
Calvary Lutheran
Minneapolis, Minnesota

- Ted Nissen
Colonial Presbyterian
Kansas City, Missouri

- Earl Paulk
Chapel Hill Harvester
Decatur, Georgia

- Kenneth Phillips
World of Pentecost
Austin, Texas

- Gordon Powell
North Main Street Church of God
Butler, Pennsylvania

- Tommy Reid
Full Gospel Tabernacle
Orchard Park, New York

- Ike Reighard
New Hope Baptist
Fayetteville, Georgia

- Ted Robinson
Central Union Church
Honolulu, Hawaii

- Arthur Rouner
Colonial Church of Edina
Edina, Minnesota

- Robert H. Schuller
Crystal Cathedral
Garden Grove, California

- David Scoates
Hennepin Avenue United Methodist
Minneapolis, Minnesota

- George Stephanides
St. Paul's Greek Orthodox
Irvine, California

- William Thompson
Trinity Lutheran
Utica, Michigan

- Morris Vaageness
North Heights Lutheran
St. Paul, Minnesota

- Lewis Vander Meer
New Community Church
Grand Rapids, Michigan

- Rick Warren
Saddleback Community
Mission Viejo, California

- Sam Williams
Del Cerro Baptist
LeMesa, California

- Joe Wright
Central Christian Church
Wichita, Kansas

- Wayne Yeager
St. Mark's Episcopal
Louisville, Kentucky

- Otis Young
First Plymouth Congregational
Lincoln, Nebraska

177

APPENDIX II

A. Information about the Board of Directors
- Number on the Board of Directors - up to twenty-five (25)
- Board Make-up
  - Nine (9) outstanding leaders from such fields as business, industry, education, medicine, etc.
  - Three (3) outstanding clergy nominated by the executive director of Churches Uniting in Global Mission (CUGM) the founding organization of RFCP.
  - Staff-members of RFCP are not eligible to serve on the board.

- Length of term - Board members serve three year terms but may be reappointed for an additional three year terms.

  For the initial board, one third of the board members will be asked to serve three years, one third will be asked to serve four year terms and one third will be asked to serve a five year term.

- Board of Directors Responsibilities

  - Appoint the Executive Director and establish a successor plan for the position.
  - Establish organizational policies for RFCP.
  - Establish fund-raising plans.
  - Review and adopt plan of work.
  - Identify and contact potential donors.
  - Develop a plan for identifying and appointing new board members.
  - Determine number and location of board meetings and the annual meeting of RFCP.
  - Review and act on operational and financial reports and recommendations.

- Expectations of Board members
  - Each board member is responsible for a minimum annual contribution to RFCP of $2,500. Each clergy board member is responsible for a minimum annual contribution of $1,000.

· Each board member to have a high interest in RFCP and to visit the Project site in Russia at least once during their term on the board.

· Active participation in board meetings and annual meeting.

Articles of Incorporation
of
Russian Farm Community Project, Incorporated
(A Not For Profit Charitable and Development Organization)

Article I

The name of the Corporation shall be Russian Farm Community Project, Incorporated.

Article II

The period of duration of the Corporation shall be perpetual unless sooner dissolved by a vote of two thirds (2/3) of the members of the Corporation in attendance at an annual meeting or a special meeting of such members called for such purposes.

Article III

The purposes for which the Corporation is organized are as follows:

To solicit and accept contributions, gifts, grants, funds and bequests of personal or real property, or both, which will be held, administered and expended to assist people in Russia, who are in transition from the old communist centrally planned system to a new market driven economy, by helping them to establish private farms and businesses, convert former state and collective farms and government operated social services into private enterprises and to establish as reliable and efficient infrastructure in support of private enterprise.

Article IV

No part of the receipts or assets of the Corporation shall inure to the benefit of or be distributable to its members, directors, or officers, provided that the Corporation may pay reasonable compensation to any person for services rendered; and no substantial part of the Corporation's activities shall consist of carrying on propaganda or otherwise attempting to influence legislation.

Article V

The members of the Corporation shall be those who contribute at least $100.00 annually to the Corporation.

Article VI

In the event of dissolution of the Corporation, the net assets of the Corporation shall be donated to a private voluntary organization doing similar development work.

Article VII

No private property or other assets of any of the members, directors, or officers of the Corporation shall ever be subject to the payment of Corporate debts to any extent whatsoever.

Article VIII

The street address of its initial registered office shall be 5223 Edina Industrial Blvd., Minneapolis, Minnesota 55439 and the name of the initial agent at such address shall be Ralph Hofstad.

Article IX

The Articles of Incorporation may be amended by a majority vote of the members of the Corporation at any annual meeting or special meeting called for that purpose, provided, however, that all amendments must have first been approved by a majority vote of the Board of Directors voting at a regular or specially called meeting of the Board.

Article X

The directors constituting the central Board of Directors shall be no more than twenty five (25) in number, and the names and street addresses of the persons who are to serve as the initial directors and of the incorporators are as follows:

181

By-Laws
of
Russian Farm Community Project Incorporated

The following by-laws are hereby adopted for and on behalf of the Russian Farm Community Project Incorporated.

Offices

1. The offices of the Corporation shall be at 5223 Edina Industrial Blvd, Minneapolis, Minnesota 55439, and as such other places as the Board of Directors may determine or the business of the Corporation may require.

Members

2. The members of the Corporation shall consist of persons who contribute at least $100.00 annually to the Corporation.

Members Meetings

3. The annual meeting of the Corporation shall be held during the first quarter of each year for the purpose of electing Directors and for the transaction of such other business as may properly come before such meeting. A ten (10) day notice of such meeting shall be given to the members. Notices should include time, date and location of meetings.

4. At all such meetings of members, those members present and entitled to vote at such meeting shall constitute a quorum for the transaction of business.

5. Special meetings of the members for any purpose may be called by the Chair of the Board of Directors at the request of the Executive Director or in writing by one-twentieth (1/20) of the members. Such a request shall state the purpose of the proposed meeting.

6. Business transacted at all special meetings shall be confined to the purpose stated in the notice thereof.

182

Directors

7. The Directors of the Corporation shall consist of no more than twenty five (25) persons elected from the membership of the Corporation at its annual meeting.

8. The Directors will serve for three years but may be re-elected to additional three year terms. There is no restriction regarding the number of terms they may serve.

9. One third of the Directors will be elected at the annual meeting each year.

10. If a Director is unable to complete his/her term, a successor may be elected by a majority of the remaining Directors. The successor shall hold office until the next election of Directors.

11. Directors, as such, shall not receive any salary for their service as Directors. This however does not preclude Directors from serving the Corporation in other capacities and receiving compensation there-for.

Meetings of the Board of Directors

12. The Board of Directors shall meet immediately following the an-nual meeting of the members to elect board officers and conduct other board business.

13. Regular meetings of the Board of Directors will be held in keeping with a schedule recommended by the Executive Director and Chair of the Corporation and ratified by the Board.

14. Special meetings of the Board of Directors may be called by the Chair.

Officers

15. Officers of the Corporation shall be elected by the Directors at the meeting of the Board of Directors immediately following the annual meeting of the members and shall consist of a Chair; Vice Chair and Secretary.

16. The Board of Directors may appoint such other officers and agents as shall be deemed necessary, who shall hold their offices for such terms, exercise such powers, and perform such duties as shall be determined from time to time by the Board of Directors.

17. The officers of the Corporation shall hold office until their successors are elected. Any officer elected or appointed by the Board of Directors may be removed at any time by the affirmative vote of the majority of the whole Board of Directors. If the office or any officer shall become vacant for any reason, the Board of Directors shall elect a successor who shall hold office for the unexpired term or until the next election of officers.

Chair

18. The Chair shall preside at meetings of the Board of Directors; shall provide leadership for the development of Board polices and see that all policies, orders and resolutions of the Board of Directors are carried out.

Vice Chair

19. The Vice Chair shall, in the absence or disability of the Chair, perform the duties and exercise the powers of the Chair and shall perform such other duties as the Board of Directors may prescribe.

Secretary

20. The Secretary shall record all board actions in official minutes of the meeting, distribute the minutes to Board members, issue notices of all regular or special meetings of the Board and membership.

Staffing

21. The Board of Directors shall contract for the services of an Executive Director who will manage the business of the corporation. The Executive Director may enter into contracts with other persons to carry out the objectives of the Corporation.

Trustees

22. There will be a Board of Trustees, consisting of those persons who contribute at least $1,000 annually to the Corporation. The Board of Trustees shall carry no official authority in the affairs of the Corporation, but may serve in an advisory capacity to the Board of Directors or staff, as requested.

Fiscal

23. The fiscal year of the Corporation shall begin on the first day of January each year.

Amendment

24. These by-laws may be amended by a majority vote at any regular meetings of the members or at any special meeting of the members, provided notice of the proposed amendment be contained in the notice of such special meeting.

APPENDIX III

MEMORANDUM OF AGREEMENT
ON COOPERATION
IN THE FIELD OF AGRICULTURAL COMPLEX
BETWEEN DMITROV DISTRICT
MOSCOW REGION ADMINISTRATION AND
CUGM RUSSIAN FARM COMMUNITY PROJECT

Dmitrov district Moscow region Administration, further named as "Administration", presented by Administration Chief Mr. V.V. Gavrilov and CUGM Russian Farm Community Project, further named as "Project", presented by it's general director Mr. Ralph Hofstad, basing on humanist principles and demonstrating mutual interest in Russian citizens life standard improvement have signed this Agreement on joint cooperation in the field of Russian agrarian reform intensification, providing growth of agricultural production and improvement of its quality.

The joint cooperation in problems, mentioned above, is to be carried out in the following directions:

CHAPTER I
SUBJECT AND GOALS OF COOPERATION

1.1.   The parts of Agreement set the task to organize eventually farms not less than 40 ha each on the base of joint stock association "Zarechenskoe" and farmers service Centre. The organized farms are to be joined into agricultural association. 5 individual farms shall be created during the first stage of mutual cooperation and the system of their cooperation with service and market enterprises will be studied. At the same time milk and vegetable processing enterprises can be established. Cooperation with existed farmers will be provided.

1.2.   The newly organized farms will be specialized in production of grain, potato, vegetables, milk, feeds and other agricultural crops in accordance with farmers desire.

1.3.   The parts of Agreement undertake the obligation to render assistance in organization and development of farms in order to provide the growth of production activities level up to international standards in the shortest possible period of time.

1.4.   The growth of agricultural production and improvement of

186

it's quality is to be obtained basing on proper use of land and other material and labour resources of plant growing and livestock-raising, new perspective varieties of agricultural crops and strains of cattle, rational use of technique, fertilizers, chemical pesticides, perfection of cattle breeding and feeding, improvement of sanitary and hygienic conditions of housing for live-stock, reduction of agricultural production losses at storage, processing, transportation and realisation as well as modern methods of farm management, crediting and financing of farms.

CHAPTER 11
CONTENT OF AGREEMENT

2.1.   Administration apportions from its reserves 2000 ha of arable lands for foundation of farms in accordance with i.l.l.(Chapter 1) of this Agreement.

2.2.   The Project carries out the control after the use of apportioned land, jointly with Administration chooses candidates for farmers, whose farms will be located on the lands of "Zarechenskoe" joint stock association.

2.3.   Inhabitants of villages, located on the apportioned lands or nearby, inhabitants of the city on Dmitrov and other towns of Dmitrov district and servicemen, transferred to reserve, may become farmers.

2.4.   In order to provide opportune and effective training of farmers for individual undertaking, Administration, Project and "Zarechenskoe" Association found the Centre of agricultural training and consulting, that besides the professional training of farmers solves tasks, mentioned in ii. 1.3 and 1.4. (Chapter 1) of this Agreement. The leading specialists of district administration as well as agrarian scientists of Moscow and suburbs educational and scientific organizations are to be enlisted to the Centre on temporary or constant base.

2.5.   In order to increase the effectiveness of the newly found farms activities the Project with assistance of Administration organizes a machine and tractor station for farmers' services milk and potato processing enterprises, on mutual consent these enterprises should be located on the territory of "Zarechenskoe" joint stock association.

2.6.   The joint stock association "Zarechenskoe" on contract base renders the farmers assistance in land cultivation, plant growing and live-stock raising, conducts purchasing, processing and marketing of agricultural production. The method of price determination will be agreed to annually.

CHAPTER III
FINANCIAL CONDITIONS

3.1.   Administration renders the newly found farms assistance in providing with necessary material resources (building materials, fertilizers, chemical pesticides, agricultural technique, etc.) for fast establishment and development of the farms.

3.2.   The Project renders financial assistance to newly established farms, machine and tractor station, milk and potato processing enterprises, other new perspective industries. For this purposes the Project uses the means of the CUGM trust fund and other possible financial sources.

3.3.   Each enterprise should pay 30% of profits to the owners. The remaining 70% share of the profits may be designated as a reserve for re-investment in the enterprise. If the other owners do not agree on future plans for the enterprise then Project can request its portion for investment in other projects in Russia.

3.4.   The Project is not intended to remove its part of profits. These means shall be included in the trust fund and reinvested in new farms or industries and improvement of economic conditions of farmers and their families.

3.5.   The Project ownership shares may be afford to sale the farmer members in a fair and reasonable manner at the beginning of each year.

CHAPTER IV
SPECIAL CONDITIONS OF AGREEMENT

4.1.   The Agreement receives power from the moment of signing and is actual for 5 years. On mutual consent it may be prolonged for a new period.

4.2.   The parts of Agreement undertake the obligation to carry out cooperation on equitable business partner basis in conditions of openness, honesty and mutual respect.

4.3.   The Agreement may be cancelled by mutual consent or by decision of one of the partners. In this case, the part, decided to cancel the Agreement, should inform the other on this not later than I year before the cancellation.

4.4.   All the labour arguments or appearing conflicts are to be solved by the parts of Agreement observing the norms of international law.

4.5.   This Agreement is draw up in Russian and English languages. Both of them have equal power.

Moscow region
Dmitrov district
Administration Chief
Signed: V.V. GAVRILOV

Russian Farm Community Project
General Director
Signed: Ralph Hofstad

"Zarechenskoe" joint stock
Association Director
Signed: V. P. Shilin

Moscow, September 20, 1993

APPENDIX IV

Memorandum of Agreement on Cooperation between
Timeryazev Agricultural Academy of Russia
and the
Russian Farms Community Project of Churches United in Global
Mission

Since 1992, the Timeryazev Agricultural Academy and the Russian Farms Community Project have cooperated in a number of activities to further their joint objectives: assisting in the privatization of Russian agriculture; improving the productivity of Russian farmers; developing a Education and Training Center to help disseminate production, management and marketing information to farmers.

It is the intent of both the Timeryazev Agricultural Academy and the Russian Farms Community Project to continue this highly productive program and to seek funds from individuals, foundations, government agencies and international organizations to support the programs in the following areas:

1. Continue and expand the research and demonstration projects for food and feed crops which will demonstrate the value of good management, high quality seed, and optimum fertilizer and plant production regimes.

2. Assist the Timeryazev Agricultural Academy with the development of an Agri-business and Extension Department which includes an undergraduate curriculum, an extension training capability and a management research program.

3. Assist the Academy to train its specialty staff in Extension service teaching.

4. Assist the Academy in the development of an integrated "Resource and Conservation Management" program which includes agricultural science, engineering and social science departments.

5. To continue to develop the Extension Education and Training Center at Ramenýe by placing resident teachers in farm man-

agement, farm accounting and agricultural marketing at the Center. This Center the Academy can use for practical training of undergraduate students and agricultural experts in Extension.

6. Develop programs which will enhance the quality of life in rural communities in Russia through improvements in the community infrastructure, health services, nutrition education and extension opportunities with the adult population of the community.

7. This agreement shall remain in force so long as it is mutually agreeable; however, either party may terminate the agreement by giving six months notice in writing to the other party.

On behalf of Russian Farms Community Projects

<Signed>

_____

Vern Moore, Deputy Executive Director

17 November 1994

On behalf of Timeryazev Agricultural Academy in Moscow

<Signed>

_____

G. Bazdyrev, Vice Rector on Education

17 November 1994

APPENDIX V

Letter of Cooperation and Understanding
between Russian Farm Community Project (RFCP) and
Administration of Dmitrov region Moscow oblast

Dmitrov   May 27, 1997

Administration of Dmitrov region Moscow oblast, hereinafter "Administration", in the person of its Head of Administration Gavrilov Valerie, and Russian Farm Community Project, hereinafter, "RFCP", in the person of its General Director Ralph Hofstad, agreed to unite their efforts of mutual collaboration with the purpose of accelerate agricultural reforms in Russia and make all agricultural type enterprises profitable and communities a desirable place to raise families.

The mutual collaboration for these activities will be carried out with four major objectives:

1.   To help Russian people take ownership of their communities and improve their economies by:
·   Creating new businesses and more jobs;
·   Creating a more efficient food and agricultural system;
·   Improving their infrastructure;
·   Developing and empowering local leadership;
·   Creating a better understanding of the free enterprise system;
·   Establishing a reliable source of credit and a better understanding of its use;
·   Providing a means for effectively accessing and utilizing appropriate technology;
·   Create a farmer-owned marketing and farm supply association.

2.   Help Russian people reconstruct their health care and social services and generally improve their quality of life with:
·   Readily accessible health care and social services at affordable prices;
·   Adequate and affordable housing.

3.   Establish the project as a model which other Russian communities can emulate:
·   Publicize program in Russia;

192

    ·   Invite Russian community leaders to visit the project;
    ·   Assist other communities in creating similar projects
in their communities.

4.   Establish a continuing Trust Fund with contributions from private and public sources in USA and Russia to implement and
sustain the project financially through its ten-year life as a model
and beyond.

Specific projects are as follow:

Farm Credit Loans

This is the third year that farms in the Dmitrov region have received
loans for crop production. We will add longer term loans for facilities,
equipment and animals this year.

Business Loans

Business loans are an expanding part of our loan portfolio and will
be increased significantly as we open later this year a business service
center in Dmitrov.

Agricultural Training and Extension Service

This important service to all farms started in 1993 and has expanded
every year. Last year a crop production specialist was employed and
this year a livestock specialist will be added to the program. This is a
major void in Russia and your government has recently initiated a commission to investigate how best to support agriculture and we all need to
support these efforts.

Dmitrov region "Distribution and Marketing Center"

To create a Distribution and Marketing Center on the basis of JSC
"Dmitrovskyi". This proposed joint venture between JSC "Dmitrovskyi"
and Russian Farm Community Project will provide a market for local
producers of agricultural products, collectives, state and private farms
in the Dmitrov region. The Russian Farms Trust Fund through its
Moscow Business Development Center will find all necessary funding
that is supported by strategic business plans and provide through this

Business Development Center in Moscow all these necessary services. Our American partners have three employees with over 100 years of experience in agricultural production and food marketing.

RFCP has already funded a 250,000 USD loan for vegetable production by «Agrodmitrov» using 500 ha of lands in JSC «Dmitrovskiy» and 100 ha at JSC «Zarechenskiy».

Before June 1 of 1997 RFCP plans to make a commitment of 1 mln. dollars to be provided to «Agrodmitrov» for the following activities:

1. Cleaning and sorting of vegetables.
2. Packaging of vegetables and production of boxes for transporting vegetables.
3. To create a marketing office.
4. To create a transportation division.
5. Make initial improvements in the storage facilities.

When this first stage is successfully completed we will start state II and raise up to 10 mln. dollars of investment funds.

Private Farmers Marketing and Supply Association

To create and support a Private Farmers Marketing association that cooperatively seeks to meet private farmers needs, for production agriculture and for marketing their production. The farmers' association should supply the farm with the necessary inputs (seeds, fertilizers, pesticides, fuel) and then collectively market their products seeking the highest return for farmers. Whenever, partnership and alliances are available they will be considered.

Added value marketing through processing

To study all means of increasing the product returns for all interested farms through added value processing. Initial emphasis will be very heavy on potato and vegetable processing with dairy and meat to follow.

Purchasing and Marketing Contracts

To study through contracting a means for all farms to work closely together voluntarily. The use of advisory committees and contracts can offer significant opportunities to reduce the costs of providing services to all agricultural enterprises with benefits achieved to be shared through the signing of contracts and to offer the users the opportunity of becoming equity owners and to participate in profit sharing.

"Zarechenskiy" Farm

RFCP will study and consider all means of addressing the financial crisis on a "Zarechenskiy' farm with the assistance of our new joint venture with "Dmitrovskyi".

Public Policy for Agriculture

Together we should hold open meetings to discuss the necessary agricultural policies that all governments put in place as they attempt to support the creation of a viable and sustainable agricultural sector. The purpose is to encourage the production of quality food at reasonable prices for all Russian consumers and seek to make Russia self-sufficient. We need a consensus on such critical issues:

- Land policy;
- Extension programs;
- Credit programs;
- Food import policies;
- Food export policies;
- Tax policies;

Three Thousand Hectares of Farm Land

The Administration of Dmitrov region will make available three thousand hectares of land for RFCP. This land to be sued for homesteading new farms and for existing farmers to increase the productivity and profitability of their operations. All funds received from the rent, sale, or lease of these land will be placed into revolving credit program and managed in Dmitrov.

Dealerships

The region urgently needs to create service centers to supply the input needs for all farms. We need everyone's support on creating model type dealerships that can provide these type of services:

- feed;
- fertilizer and chemicals'

- seeds;
- equipment;
- others.

RFCP will seek and find suppliers to partner with to create these farm supply service centers. Success here will be a model that can be replicated throughout Russia. We have initiated discussion with four major agri-business corporations and next week our third meeting will be held in Amsterdam.

Local Leadership

To fulfill the above objectives it is necessary to have support from local leaders. We want to recognize the following people and all others that have been advisors and friends.

·	Head of local Administration:	V. Gavrilov
·	Director of JSC "Dmitrovskyi":	F. Azorkin
·	Director of "Bunyatino" agrofirm:	V. Krilov
·	Director of JSC "Ramenýe:	M. Osipov
·	Board of Directors of FMA:	1. I. Terekhina
		2. V. Soloviev
		3. N. Moskvin
		4. A. Butchin
		5. N. Nocolaev
·	Russian Director of RFCP:	A. Danilenko
·	Dmitrov Director of RFCP:	L. Remenev
·	Technical Advisor of RFCP:	V. Storozhenko
·	Community Administration:	A. Drovninova

With the support of such local leaders our project will not fail. With God's blessing we will do our best to achieve all of these goals and objectives for Russian agriculture and the rural communities.

Summary Statement

We are a non-profit Russian entity committed to using all of our funds in Russian projects. All profits for loans and investments are recycles through the audited Trust Fund. Helping people to help themselves is our objective and in the new market economy in Russia they need the assistance of a private sector infra-structure. We trust the Russian government will continue to study how best they can do their part and recognize that quality low cost food in all of the western countries was assisted significantly by meaningful, helpful government programs. The support from the Dmitrov Raion has been very much appreciated and trust all other government entities will do likewise. The Administration of Dmitrov Raion pledges to be an example of how the private sector and government can become partners and successfully respond to the needs of its people.

Head of Dmitrov
Administration

_____

V. Gavrilov

General Director
of RFCP

_____

R. Hofstad

Russian Director
of RFCP

_____

A. Danilenko

APPENDIX VI

Agreement
between Russian Farm Community Project (USA) and
Administration of Dmitrov region, Moscow Oblast (Russia)
on Public-Private Partnership for
economic growth through regional investment

December 10, 1997   Dmitrov

Administration of Dmitrov region, Moscow oblast (Russia), in the person of the Head of Administration, Valerie Gavrilov, and Russian Farm Community Project (USA), in the person of its Executive Director Ralph Hofstad and Director Andrei Danilenko, hereinafter "parties",

·   being encouraged to achieve objectives identified in the Letter of Cooperation and understanding signed by the parties on May 27, 1997,

·   acknowledging the success of the third year of credit leading program and five-years training and consulting activities for farmers in the region,

·   recognizing capital investments and know-how resources as critical components required to actualize economic potential of the region,

agreed on the principles of public-private partnership for economic growth in the region through creation and utilization f favorable investment environment and collaboration of public and private sector on the following objectives:

1.   Create a favorable investment environment in the region with adequate incentives for both domestic and foreign capital.

2.   By means of necessary information, capital, modern technology and management tools assist improvement of efficiency and

competitiveness of existing enterprises, development of a newly established private enterprises which would contribute to sustainable economic development of the region, create new jobs and growth opportunities.

3. Establishing model operation in Dmitrov region, <u>demonstrate</u> to the global and domestic financial and corporate community the commercial viability of investments in the sphere of agribusiness in Russia.

For the purposes of achieving identified objectives the parties have agreed on the following actions and commitments:

Objective N° 1

Administration of Dmitrov region:

· Develop a system of tax breaks and other incentives for capital investment projects, subject to this agreement;

· Provide technical assistance for capital investment projects, subject to this agreement;

· Provide financial assistance and partial funding of selected projects, subject to this agreement;

· Identify capital needs and respective investment opportunities of the region;

· Consider participation in selected investment projects by the means of providing ownership, equity or debt tools;

· Provide necessary and reasonable guarantees to selected investment projects, subject to this agreement;

· Represent interests of regional investments in matters, subject to federal laws and regulations:

· Provide any other assistance, as deemed necessary and appropriate.

Objective Nº 2

Russian Farm Community Project, in conjunction with International Fund "Russian Farms" (Russia) and Business Development Center (Russia):

· Identify and assess investment opportunities;

· Develop investment proposals and provide business and financial planning for identified projects;

· Conduct feasibility studies, provide any other relevant research and expertise, required for projects preparation and implementation;

· Provide its own debt and equity financing for projects, meeting the established investment criteria and guidelines;

· Develop strategic business partnerships and alliances to bring capital investments, modern technology and management practices;

· Source outside financing based on the needs of each project by working with international financial organizations, institutional and corporate investor;

· Develop a system of financial and management control for the investment projects, subject to this memorandum.

Objective Nº 3

The parties have agreed to unite efforts in promoting and publicizing the experiences of the present regional public-private initiative, aimed at creation of a meaningful link between public and private sector in creating a favorable business and investment environment to achieve greater economic growth and prosperity. The parties will seek to promote investment opportunities in the region by addressing domestic and corporative community.

Final Comments

For the purpose of effectively executing the present agreement, the parties have agreed to establish a Public-Private Advisory Commission with the responsibility to develop specific recommendations on the implementations on the implementation of the above listed actions and continuously monitor current progress.

In addition, the parties have agreed to consider the establishment of a Business Development Center in Dmitrov region that could be instrumental in facilitating critical business activities, required to successfully achieve the objectives of the present agreement.

Head of Administration of Dmitrov region, Moscow oblast (Russia)
<Signed>

_____

V.V. Gavrilov

Executive Director, Russian Farm Community Project (USA)
<Signed>

_____

Ralph P. Hofstad

Director, Russian Farm Community Project, Moscow (Russia)
<Signed>

_____

Andrei L. Danilenko

APPENDIX VII

MEMORANDUM OF AGREEMENT
BETWEEN
TIMERYAZEV AGRICULTURAL ACADEMY
THE RUSSIAN FARM COMMUNITY PROJECT
AND THE UNIVERSITY OF MINNESOTA
COLLEGE OF AGRICULTURAL, FOOD,
AND ENVIRONMENTAL SCIENCES

October 5, 1998

Introduction

Since 1992, the Timeryazev Agricultural Academy in Moscow, Russia and the Russian Farm Community Project have cooperated in a number of activities to further their joint objectives: assisting in the privatization of Russian agriculture; improving the productivity of Russian farmers; and developing an education and training center as well as an extension effort to help disseminate production, management and marketing information to farmers.

Purpose

The Timeryazev Agricultural Academy the Russian Farm Community project, and the College of Agricultural, Food, and Environmental Sciences of the University of Minnesota, St. Paul, Minnesota, U.S. hereby and herein acknowledge the addition of the University of Minnesota into this effort for the purpose of expanding the educational offerings for Russian farmers by establishing a collaborative agricultural training and extension program between he Timeryazev Agricultural Academy and the University of Minnesota.

The agreement is intended to facilitate the development of the following kinds of collaboration which are of mutual interest and benefit to the three parties:

·   faculty exchanges
·   exchange of scientific information
·   collaborative training programs
·   collaborative research

In addition, because of the importance of the teaching missions of Timeryazev Agricultural Academy and the University of Minnesota, they hereby further agree to explore and promote opportunities for two-way student exchanges.

It is understood by all parties that this Agreement does not commit funds from either institution and that implementation of the collaborative efforts envisioned depends on the availability of funding, both external as well as internal.

Procedures

Each party will designate a coordinating office and primary contact person to facilitate communications. The languages of communication are Russian and English.

Once initiated, each project or area of collaboration will be guides by a work plan and budget developed jointly each year by the three parties and preceded by a review of the previous years activities and accomplishments.

A joint annual report will be prepared summarizing activities and accomplishments realized under the auspices of this Agreement.

The initial project of collaboration selected by mutual agreement of all parties will focus on the dairy sector as described below. It is understood that specific projects and programs will be developed in other areas as needs are identified and resources become available.

Dairy Management Training

The proposed Dairy Management Training Program will concentrate on the most important missing link in the industry by introducing a dairy management training and management know-how component as well as specific management tools (dairy management software), which will be instrumental in training and educational efforts.

The goal of the program is to disseminate the knowledge of modern dairy management practices in Russia, which will lead to sustainable and profitable dairy operations.

The program will have the following objectives:

1.   Develop a training program for trainers, designed and delivered by dairy management faculty/staff of Timeryazev Agricultural Academy in conjunction with the University of Minnesota and dairy business experts. The 3-4 Russian candidates selected will acquire theoretical, practical and methodological knowledge and skills through a 2-month long intensive dairy management training program in the United States.

        Expected outcomes: This specially tailored program will equip Russian dairy trainers with the latest dairy management knowledge and extension training skills in the areas of Agronomy, Nutrition and Feeding, Reproduction and Genetic Selection, Lactation and Milking, Raising Dairy Heifers, and Dairy Farm Business Management.

2.   Develop a training program for dairy farm workers and managers from Russia, including hands-on practical training at farms in the United States. Selected cohorts (7-10 trainees in each cohort annually for the period of three years) of Russian dairy workers and managers will be brought to the United States to complete four (4) months of on-farm training and two (2) weeks of intensive management technique training in a classroom setting.

        Expected outcomes: The participants will gain skills required o operate a successful and profitable dairy farm in the positions of Agronomist; Nutrition and Feeding Technician; Custom Heifer Raising Technician; Reproduction and Genetic Selection Technician; and Dairy Farm Business Manager.

3.   Make dairy management software (Dairy Champ) available o trainers and trainees in the Russian language, fully adaptable o Russian dairy conditions.

        Expected outcomes: The software should have full operational capabilities and sufficient training capabilities with extensive portfolio of help menus. The participants of the program will be training to use this dairy management software and understand the operational reports which it generates.

4.   Develop an on-going, on-site training program in Russia which would be designed to disseminate the knowledge and experience gained during the first phase of the project.

Expected outcomes: On-site extension classes will bring the knowledge to dairy farmers in Russia with anticipated annual turnout of 100 attendees. At least two demonstration farms will provide practical learning opportunities for interested Russian dairy farmers.

It is the intent of the three parties to develop a joint proposal and seek funds from individuals, foundations, government agencies and international organizations to underwrite this collaborative effort in Dairy Management Training.

The effective date of this Agreement is October 5, 1998. The agreement shall remain in force so long as it is mutually agreeable; however, either party may terminate the Agreement by giving six (6) months notice in writing to the other party. Having read the present Agreement and being fully aware of the content, the parties hereby affix their signatures.

On Behalf of the Russian Farm Community Project

Signed: Ralph Hofstad
               Executive Director

Signed: Andrei Danilenko
               Project Director (Russia)

On Behalf of the Timeryazev Agricultural Academy

Signed: Anatoly Puponin
               Rector

Signed: Victor Storozhenko, Head
               Department of Foreign Studies

Signed: Yuri Isilov, Professor
               Department of Dairy Science

On Behalf of the University of Minnesota
College of Agricultural, Food, and Environmental Sciences

Signed: Philip Larsen, Interim Dean and
                 Vice President for Agricultural Policy

Signed: Gerald Miller, Associate Dean, Extension

Signed: Steven Clarke, Acting Director,
                 International Agricultural Programs

APPENDIX VIII

Mission Statement

"The Business Development Center Partner Ltd. will provide professional services and management for new and existing companies. The Business Development Center will assist Russian and foreign companies through their registration, start-up and/or growth that will assure success to both."

Executive Summary

A.   Overview:

The Business Development Center "Partner" is organized as a wholly owned subsidiary of the International Fund "Russian Farms" (Trust Fund) and Russian Farm Community Project (RFCP), and its purpose will be to assist new and existing business to grow and become profitable. "Partner" will actively pursue new clients, Russian and foreign, to contract for services and space.

To accomplish the above, the RFCP will transfer the operating and administrative functions to the BDC as of September 1, 1998. The transfer will include all personnel, equipment, furniture and vehicles to the BDC. The BDC will provide and charge for services at rates shown in the Marketing Strategy section. All client services will be performed under contracts and leases with clients will be standardized (Attachment 4). It is important to clearly understand the relationship between the BDC and its various clients, for example:

1.   "Each client/tenant will retain its own identity, authority, and responsibility for decision making functions".

2.   Request for services must be clearly stated and understood by both parties.

3.   Clients/tenants will retain their own bank accounts, but may contract with the BDC to perform accounting services, bank reconciliation and periodic financial reports.

4.   Policy and business strategies will be the responsibility of the

client/tenant and not of BDC personnel. BDC may contract 'to perform certain services on behalf of its client/tenant such as Research, Marketing, Business Plans, feasibility study, legal services and others, but the final decision making authority rests with the Client/tenant.

5. Financial accounting will be performed to Russian Accounting Standards and in western style "GAAP" format.

6. All client information will be confidential.

7. Clients/tenants will be billed for services on a monthly basis and must promptly pay upon invoicing.

8. BDC personnel will initially be assigned to projects familiar to them prior to their transfer, however, as future work loads develop and skills are improved, they may be assigned o multiple projects or advance to supervisory position.

9. The BDC will operate under the organizational chart as approved and dated by management (Attachment 2). All jobs will be performed as outlined in their respective job descriptions Performance evaluations will be conducted periodically, but not less then once a year, based on the job descriptions. Pay for performance program will be developed in the first year of operating. A wage and salary plan should be adopted that would reflect a high, low and medium pay range based on performance, tenure and level of responsibility. A pay differential of 5-10% should be adopted that would reflect the increased requirements of supervisory personnel. Maintain a minimum number of incremental levels of authority.

10. The BDC will operate as an independent, for profit business. Formal operating policies will be developed to streamline and standardize office operations. Although operating policies are dynamic and subject to regular changes, the initial set of policies will be ready for management's review and comments no later then October 15, 1998. Upon management's initial approval these policies will be reviewed periodically, but not less then once a year, by the Human Recourse director. Proposed

changes, if any, must be approved and dated by the General Manager. Copies of policies will be provided to each employee initially and minor changes will be provided as addendum.

11.   Certain staff members and employees may be assigned on a full time basis to individual clients/tenants and their time and services will be billed accordingly. Those employees/staffers serving multiple clients/tenants will be required to maintain daily time sheets in 15 minute increments and deliver them to the accounting department for processing and billing to the various client/tenant.

B.   Implementation:

To accomplish the above will require a sequentially phased implementation plan. The proposed sequence is as follows:

1.   An initial orientation phase, should begin with a carefully presented description of the plans intent, including:

- potential growth;
- organizational structure;
- respect for General Director's time; and
- career opportunities.

It is imperative that this plan be clearly understood by all employees. Particular attention should be given to reporting structure, lines of authority and responsibility (estimated time minimum 2 weeks).

2.   An intensive training program for accountants must be implemented by well qualified instructors to develop and install a uniform system of accounting based on GAAP, preferably the Great Plains accounting package presently used by Crystal Cathedral (estimated time 3 months).

3.   Develop a strategic marketing plan that will focus on understanding space and/or services. This may be designed and implemented in house, if qualified staff is available. It may be more cost-effective to contract for these services by independent consultants such as Pavel Gagarin.

4.   Subsequent phases may be initiated as needs arise.

C.   Prospects for Success:

Management believes that the current financial situation is, of course, worrisome, but the long-term outlook for Russia is still bright. The main founders, the Trust Fund/RFCP are committed to success and will provide the financial and technical skills to be successful.

The ultimate success of "Partner" will be its management's ability to:

(1)   maintain a high-level of occupancy;
(2)   control cost; and
(3)   to effectively attract outside clients for consulting services.

The General Director, *Mr. Andrei Danilenko,* through his work as President of the International Fund "Russian Farms" has built an effective Moscow networking system that will be invaluable to the BDC as a means for attracting new clients. In addition, the stated BDC organization structure will help Mr. Danilenko delegate responsibility and authority to other qualified staff members, freeing himself to better and more effectively manage the BDC.

The leadership for financial control will be provided by *Mr. Muslim Umiryaev.* Mr. Umiryaev is currently financial controller of the trust Fund, but his duties will be transferred to the BDC.

Mr. Umiryaev has proven himself to be quite effective in the area of internal cost accounting and his skill in this area should conservatively save the BDC from 10 - 15% in cost savings.

It is planned that the new organization will be profitable from the start of operation. The plan presented is for the period September 1998 through December 1999. In that time the BDC is expected to achieve profit base of $17,989 in the remaining months of 1998, and $73,877 in 1999. The profit margins are expected to be 8.0% the first year, and rise to 10.0% the next year.

APPENDIX IX

THE AGREEMENT
of Social Program Development in Dmitrov Region Between Dmitrov Region Administration and Russian Farm Community Project

Moscow   7, December, 1999

Dmitrov Region Administration on behalf of Gavrilov V.V., the Head of the Administration, and Russian Farm Community Project on behalf of Danilenko A. L. the President of the International Fund "Russian Farms", hereinafter referred as "parties", on basis of the Letter of Cooperation and Understanding between parties from May 27, 1997, have concluded the present agreement as follows:

According to the above-stated Letter, one of directions of activity of the Russian Farm Community Project is the assistance to Dmitrov Region Administration in development of social sphere in Region and health care system. The purpose is level of live improving, maintenance of constant access to the health system and social services.

The above stated parties herein agree to pursue the project initiatives as listed below through collaborative efforts and fulfill all obligations as stipulated in progress attachments.

1.   **RFCP:** Raising $ 100,000 for the construction of an elderly transitional housing, facility that will connect with the House of Kindness in Dmitrov to provide services of housing, daycare and outreach services.

2.   **RFCP:** To render the humanitarian help in supply of medical establishments in Dmitrov region (local medical clinics, hospital) medical equipment (second-hand good condition) and medicines from USA.

3.   **RFCP and Dmitrov Region Administration:** To continue Joint Youth Program development according to the TUG and TUG(R) Projects.

4.   **RFCP:** To render the humanitarian help with transport for health care.

211

5.   **RFCP:** To secure funds for purchase of equipment for teenagers recreation center.

6.   **RFCP:** To continue funding efforts for remodeling of the church in village Ramenie of Dmitrov region. **Dmitrov Region Administration:** provide all necessary support to complete the project.

7.   **RFCP and Dmitrov Region Administration:** To find possibilities to develop Youth Drug Prevention Program, created by joint efforts.

Due to this new Agreement, the Agreement between Dmitrov Region Administration and Russian Farm Community Project dated May 7, 1998 is terminated

Head of Dmitrov Region
Signed: V.V. Gavrilov

RFCP Representative -RFCP Director Administrator
Signed: Vern Moore

International Fund "Russian Farms" President
Signed: A.L. Danilenko

ATTACHMENT NO. I

Construction of Transitional Care Facility
as Connected to the House of Kindness in Dmitrov

7 December 1999

In accordance with the Agreement of Social Program development in Dmitrov region between Dmitrov Region Administration and Russian Farm Community Project (RFCP) signed on

1.　　RFCP on behalf of International Fund Russian Farms with Dmitrov Administration will work cooperatively to construct a transitional facility for the elderly and disabled (invalids). The building design and contraction will include features which support the concept of a "model facility" for access and living (conditions) for disable persons.

2.　　Dmitrov Administration agrees to provide construction preliminary plan in order to put it at American side disposal in an attempt to raise funds for the construction.

Final Project documentation, which will be turned over by the Administration has to include the following:
a)　　general plan and landscape drawing
b)　　building construction blue prints to be completed by February 1, 2000
c)　　communication layouts, sewage, water and electric
d)　　construction costs of building; interior and exterior

3.　　Dmitrov Administration agrees to select a contractor by competitive basis. The contractor is obligated to provide the Administration with timetable of constriction from start to finish.

4.　　Administration of Dmitrov shall be obligated to provide financing of construction project above and beyond $ 1 00,000 - to the stage of operations.

213

5.　　　RFCP will raise $100,000 for contribution toward the construction, over a period of 2 years. January 1, 2000 - December 31, 2001.

6.　　　All funds raised by RFCP will be transmitted through the International Fund "Russian Farms". International Fund "Russian Farms" will help coordinate the project for RFCP.

7.　　　Dmitrov Administration will designate a project coordinator who will make monthly reports to RFCP office in Moscow. Moscow office will translate the report and send it to RFCP in Minneapolis, USA.

Head of Dmitrov Region
Signed: V.V. Gavrilov

RFCP Representative - RFCP Director Administration
Signed: Vern L. Moore

RFCP Representative - International Fund "Russian Farms" President
Signed: A.L. Danilenko

ATTACHMENT NO. 2

Health Care Initiatives between RFCP and Dmitrov Region Administration

In accordance with the Agreement of Social Program development in Dmitrov region between Dmitrov Region Administration and Russian Farm Community Project (RFCP) signed on 7 December, 1999.

1.   RFCP and International Fund "Russian Farms" will render the humanitarian help in supply of medical institutions of the region with:

1.1.   Solicit Donations of Drugs From US Manufacturers:
-       Insulin: Humulin in Cartridges
-       Cephalosporins for intravenous use
-       Oncology Drugs
-       Vaccines: Hepatitis B
                       Hepatitis A
                       Measles, Mumps, Rubella (MMR)
- Multivitamin and Fluoride Supplements

1.2.   Solicit Donations of Durable Hospital Equipment:
-       30 examination tables for newborns
-       100 overbed tables
-       40 drug storage cabinets
-       2 defibrillators for ambulances
-       15 electrocardiography machines with battery chargers
-       5 + commodes
-       10 wheelchairs
-       25 manually adjustable beds
-       15 walkers
-       1 manual transport (Hoyer) lift
-       2 physiotherapy exercise machines
-       transfer board
Basic lab equipment for Feldschar clinics, e.g. blood and urine testing,
-       Bilirubin testing equipment for newborn

1.3.   Solicit Donations of Disposable Hospital Equipment

- X ray film
- Syringes and needles, various sizes
- Intravenous supplies and tubing
- Blood donation equipment
- Lab coats, masks, gloves
- Air-inflated splints of different sizes
- Neck braces

Administration of Dmitrov Region will distribute the donations in accordance with the demand.

2.   RFCP and Dmitrov Region Administration will initiate Exchange Program for Health, Social Work Professionals:

2.1.   Group of 6 representative medical specialists from US to visit Dmitrov region.

2.2.   Group of Dmitrov 4 health and 2 social work professionals to visit comparable institutions in Minnesota.

Head of Dmitrov Region
Signed: V.V. Gavrilov

RFCP Representative - RFCP Director Administration
Signed: Vern L. Moore

RFCP Representative - International Fund "Russian Farms" President
Signed: A.L. Danilenko

ATTACHMENT NO. 3

Cooperation in the field of Youth policy

7 December 1999

In accordance with the Agreement of Social program development in Dmitrov region between Dmitrov Region Administration and Russian Farm Community Project (RFCP) signed on

1.	RFCP and Administration. Organize the Youth Exchange and Training pro-rams between the US and Dmitrov region teens and Young Adults on an annual basis.

2.	RFCP. Provides training for the Young People in the 40 assets program.

3.	RFCP and Administration. Assist the Youth Department of Dmitrov Administration in Drug prevention program.

4.	RFCP and Administration. Establish regular exchange of information with the US Youth through the Internet.

5.	RFCP and Administration. Develop a program which could assist the Dmitrov region Youth with career orientation.

Head of Dmitrov Region
Signed: V.V. Gavrilov

RFCP Representative - RFCP Director Administration
Signed: Vern L. Moore

RFCP Representative - International Fund "Russian Farms" President
Signed: A.L. Danilenko

APPENDIX X

MEMORANDUM

on cooperation of the Russian Farm Community Project (USA), the International Fund "Russian Farms"with the International Foundation for Socio-Economic and Political Studies (Russia)

The Russian Farm Community Project (RFCP),The International Fund "Russian Farms" (DW) and the International Foundation for Socio-Economic and Political Studies (Gorbachev Foundation) hereinafter referred to as "Sides",

·   coming from mutual desire to establish mutually beneficial co-operation;
·   believing that cooperation of the Sides will be mutually beneficial;
·   taking into account accumulated experience and positive results of U. S. Russian cooperation in agricultural field;
·   noting high level of results of cooperation undertaking in the Dmitrovsky Raion of the Moscow oblast in the framework of the RFCP agricultural programs;
·   taking into account the interest to establish the Public Partnership Agreement under which the Sides will be able to participate actively in the process of revival of the agricultural section of the Russian economy;

Have agreed on following:

Article 1.

Cooperation in the framework of this Memorandum will be carried through in accordance with acting laws, rules and procedures of both countries and will contribute to development of interaction in areas, determined by agreement on the basis of equality, reciprocity and mutual benefit.

Article 2.

Sides will encourage cooperation by exchange ideas, information, experience, technologies, conducting seminars and meetings, implementation of joint projects, training and retraining personnel and other mutually agreed forms of cooperation.

Article 3.

The objective of this memorandum is arranging the Side's active cooperation in agricultural sector for revival existing agricultural complex and development a new system of Farm Community in Russia involving restructuring and bringing profitability former state farms through the use of good management practices relating to production, financing, marketing and personnel. It implies the use of "model of success" achieved in the Dmitrov Raion in creation of the support system for farms in particular through the Farm Supply and Services Center.

Article 4.

The sides determine and elaborate fields of cooperation in accordance with this Memorandum.

Gorbachev Foundation:
·provide support to revitalizing processes for certain agricultural areas. As a first step is recommended Krasnogvardej ski Raion of the Stavropolsky krai;
·execute contacts with corresponding governmental organizations in Russia, in the USA and with other interested countries;
·provide necessary assistance to its partners;
·participate in working out by WU issues of the creation the Development Fund, specialized in direct investment to the Russian agricultural complex;
·together with RFCP and with the Trust Fund is taking measures to seek funds for the joint projects on development of agricultural complex in Russia and in the first turn in Krasnogvardeiski Raion;
·making research on issues mutually agreed by the Sides, including strategies for solving world food issues.

RFCP and IFRF
·promote the Dmitrov "model of success' to other regions of Russia;
·as a first important step could be creation in these regions Farm Supply Centers. Its mission to become the premier provider of stable

credit supply of agricultural complex, supply of agricultural goods and services for the agricultural producers in these regions. Its strategy is to build long term relationship with farmers by providing quality products, training, and other support services.

Article 5.

Cooperation of the sides will be carried through on the basis of protocols and additional arrangements in accordance with agreed programs of activities by which stages, terms and other conditions will be determined. Such protocols and additional arrangements will correspondingly determine subjects, procedures, financial conditions and other issues of cooperation.

Article 6.

Cooperation will be carried through in different forms including:
provision of effective interaction with corresponding organizations, including the local Administration, the Government of the Russian Federation, the Russian Academy of Sciences, the Timeryzev Agricultural Academy with the aim to receive support for activities in this field from corresponding organizations in Russia and in the USA;
selection candidates and carrying joint interviews with an aim to evaluate professional levels of farmers and other agricultural specialists;
development training and retraining programs of farm managers and other technical personnel;
creation of grand system and its services for provision grands to candidates for participation in system of training and retraining of Russian specialists;
carrying out programs of training, retraining and provision certification to farm managers and technical personnel, including short-term and long-term courses in Russia and in the USA;

Article 7.

For purpose of effective realization of this Memorandum the sides set up the joint working group, objectives of which will be the following:
consideration and development recommendations on issues related

to creation of the most favorable conditions for carrying cooperation;

·provide support to mechanisms for exchange information, consultative activities, as well as training and retraining personnel;

·evaluation of results and development recommendations to improve cooperation;

·discussion of the issues, related to cooperation between sides, consideration of which will be recommended by the working group.

Article 8.

For realization of cooperation in the framework of this Memorandum and taking into consideration of international commitments, national laws and rules, each side takes the following obligations:

·promote entry to its territory and exit corresponding collaborators of the side, as well as import and export equipment of other side, used in projects and programs in the framework of this Memorandum;

·provide organization of programs of joint activities, training and retraining personnel, meetings, acquaintance visits, which let collaborators of the side, who participate in cooperation in the framework of this Memorandum, carry out events foreseen by the programs, including passage to corresponding geographic places, visit the necessary entities, acquaintance with data and materials of practical interest for cooperation, contacts separate specialists necessary for implementation of this measures.

·promote tax free import of necessary materials and equipment, foreseen by this Memorandum to use in joint programs and projects.

Organizing issues, rising during activity foreseen by this article could be considered by the working group, which will develop recommendations for its solution.

Article 9.

The sides will aspire to avoid any arguments and discords in relation to explication and implementation of this Memorandum and in case of its emerging to solve by bilateral negotiations.

Article 10

The Memorandum enters into force at the moment of its signature by both sides and will be in force during three years. It could be changed and extended for next five year periods on joint sides written agreement.

The action of this Memorandum could be stopped at any time by any side by written notification to other side before three months.

Discontinuation of activities of this Memorandum will not effect implementation of any cooperation, implementing in the framework of this Memorandum and not completed at the moment of its discontinuation of action.

Signed in _____ 1999 in two copies each in English and Russian, both copies have the same power.

For the Russian Farm Community Project
Signed: Ralph Hofstad

For the International Fund "Russian Farms"
Signed: Andrei Danilenko

For International Foundation for SocioEconomic and Political Studies
Signed: M. Gorbachev

December 17, 1999

Attachment to the Memorandum

on cooperation of the Russian Farm Community Project (USA), the International Fund "Russian Farms" with the International Foundation for Socio-Economic and Political Studies (Russia).

By this Attachment is determined the plan of interaction of the International Foundation for Socio-Economic and Political Studies, the Administration of the Krasnogvardjski raion of the Stavropolski Krai with the International Fund "Russian Farms" and with the Corporation "Russian Farm Project" hereafter referred to as "Sides", with an objective to prepare proposals on cooperation in the field of development of the agricultural complex of the Krasnogvardejski raion of the Stavropolki kri.

In accordance with the memorandum on cooperation of the Russian Farm Community project (USA), the International Fund "Russian Farms" with the International Foundation for Socio-Economic and Political Studies the Sides confirm its intention to form up a number of the joint projects, implementation of which would be carried out with taking into consideration of the accumulated experience and reached results of the activities of the International Fund "Russian Farms" in the Dmitrov raion of the Moscow region.

For this objective it is proposed the following stages of activities:

·in January, 2000 make a meeting of the corresponding specialists during which to discuss, in a preliminary way, a format and a contend of the proposed for cooperation of the joint projects, taking into account the proposals of the Administration of the Krasnogvardejski raion of the Stavropolski krai;

·at the end of January or at the beginning of the February 2000 organize Mr. M. Gorbachev visit to the Dmitrov raion with the aim to make acquaintance with the reached results in the framework of the programs of the "Russian Community Project" and of the International Fund "Russian Farms" addressed to revitalization of the agroindustrial

223

complex if this raion.

·in February 2000 organize a mission of the group of specialists to the Krasnogvardeiski raion of the Stavroposki krai to study conditions for formation possible joint agricultural projects;

·at the end of February 2000 on the basis of results of the above mission prepare an investment program for the cooperation of the proposed join projects and the proposals for seeking financial means needed for implementation of these projects;

·in March - April 2000 in Moscow held a meeting to approve the proposed for cooperation the joint projects and the fund raising measures.
·in case of the successful fund raising operation in the period of the Easter (beginning of May 2000) it is proposed to organize Mr. M.S. Gorbachev visit together with two or three specialists to the Krasnogvardeiski raion for a ticker-tape reception to open activities of the first investment projects.

·at the fall of the 2000 it is proposed to foreseen possibilities of Mr. M. Gorbachev visit to the U.S.A. During the visit it is suggested to organize his meetings with the potential U.S. partners, as well as to make his speeches at the Universities and other organizations on the modern tendency in the Russian economy and in the Agriculture as well as on possibilities which Russia could have from the cooperation in this field.

For the Russian Farm Community Project
Signed: Ralph Hofstad

For International Fund "Russian Farms"
Signed: F. Danilenko

For International Fund for Socio-Economic and Political Studies
Signed: M. Gorbachev

For Administration of the Krasnogvardejski raion of the Stavropolski krai
Signed: S. Belich